LETTERS TO THE EDITOR

A MISCELLANY

FROM THE PAGES OF

COUNTRY LIFE

LETTERS TO THE EDITOR
A MISCELLANY

❉

FROM THE PAGES OF
COUNTRY LIFE

COUNTRY LIFE EDITOR MARK HEDGES

COMPILED AND EDITED BY SAM CARTER
SERIES CONSULTANT JOHN GOODALL

SIMON &
SCHUSTER
ILLUSTRATED

London · New York · Sydney · Toronto · New Delhi

A CBS COMPANY

First published in Great Britain by Simon & Schuster UK Ltd, 2012
A CBS COMPANY

1 3 5 7 9 10 8 6 4 2

SIMON & SCHUSTER
ILLUSTRATED BOOKS
Simon & Schuster UK Ltd
222 Gray's Inn Road
London
WC1X 8HB

www.simonandschuster.co.uk

Simon & Schuster Australia, Sydney

Simon & Schuster India, New Delhi

Series Editor and Project Manager: Sam Carter
Series Consultant: John Goodall
Country Life Picture Library Manager: Justin Hobson
Designer: Two Associates/Richard Proctor
Literary Agent: Jonathan Conway, Mulcahy Conway Associates

A CIP catalogue record for this book is available from the British Library

ISBN 978-1-84983-832-0

Printed and bound by CPI Group (UK) Ltd, Coydon, CR0 4YY

CONTENTS

FOREWORD BY MARK HEDGES ix

1. "CAN THE READER ADVISE?" 1

Do Dogs See Ghosts? • Floating Golf Balls • Milk Bottle Cap Cut Open
by Tits • Feeding Kinkajous • Do Dogs Think? • Cider and Rheumatism
• "A" or "An" • Shoeing the Goose • Berries Foretelling a Hard Winter •
Savage Australian Black Swan • What Have I Found? • To Keep off
Tramps • Gold-fish Losing Colour • Lizards as Pets • The Effect
of Music on Dogs

2. "HAVE YOU SEEN?" 29

Si Fractus Illabatur Orbis • Fire-fighting • An Interesting Relic •
Old-time Dancing • St. Distaff's Day • The Church's Humbler Servants
• Wasp Scissors • An Accident in Canada • A Wool Train in the Lakes •
The Evolution of the Golf Ball • Cricket Bats • Attitudes of Footballers
• A London Pet • How an Invalid Read the Wind

3. "CAN THE EDITOR ADVISE?" 51

Four-legged Golf Caddie • A Curious Coincidence • Harmful Snakes
in England • A Quaint Custom • An Interesting Freak • What is
Unwomanliness? • To Prevent Moths • A Difficult Question • Frogs
by Rail • Old Billiard Rules • Lost Golf Ball Law • Dry Gut in Tennis
Rackets • To Find a Dead Rat in a House • On £500 a Year! • Country
Headquarters • Noises in a New House • Physical Deterioration •
Fresh Air v. Draughts • Monkeys as Pets • Meerkats • A Regimental Pet

4. "I can recommend" 85

The Law and the Burglar • Dog's Death from Chicken Bone •
Measuring Height of Trees • Dew Collecting • Colonial Intercourse
• Cure for Warts • To Outwit Flies and Midges • Sneezing • Suggestion
for Collecting Rain Water • Haycutting up to Date • Stoolball • Revival
of the Game of Quintain • "Modern Maid's Uniform" • Postillion v.
Coachman • Some Delusions Regarding Oysters • Marking Trails •
The Van Cottage

5. Country Life at War 113

Wounded Horses in War • Often Wounded • Russian Peasantry and
War • The Russian's Prayer for his Horse • "Country Life" at the Front
• Home Again • Letters from a Subaltern • Within Sound of the Guns
• A Lamb's War Service • Ladies at Greenwich • From a Prisoner in
Germany • Turn Out Your Paper • Back Numbers of "Country Life"

6. The Reader's Voice 135

The Reader Responds • Lawn Tennis at its Highest • Women as Railway
Officials • A Relic of a Doomed Line • The Premonition of Storms by
Birds and Animals • The Last Bath Chair • An Unfledged Cuckoo in
August • London Spring • Dog Stealing • Golf Courtesy • Shoes of the
Great • Wild Birds' Eggs for Food • "Country Life" • Hay Fever • The
First Snowdrop • Voyages on Some Scotch Rivers • Frogs as Weather
Indicators • Old Field Names • The Padstow Hobby-horse Dance •
Yorkshire Sword Dancers • Barlow Well Dressing • The Cuckoo's Tune
• Boggarts, Fairies and Running Water • The Eton v. Harrow match
• A Primitive Ferry

7. "It might amuse your readers to know" 173

Diving Dogs • The Odds against Thirteen Trumps • Earwigs in the House • Coins in Potatoes • A Strange Resurrection • A Police Station in a Tree • Self-sacrifice! • Minds Other than Ours • The Bray of the Ass • Musical Phrase in Blackbird's Song • A Tame Squirrel • Monstrous Rabbit's Teeth • A Dog Who Plays Croquet • A Rhinoceros as a Pet • Singing Mice • A Cure for Gout and Rheumatism

8. Local Types 191

A Sussex Centenarian • A Child of Nature • The Village Cobbler • An Undistressed Irishman • Argyllshire Gipsies • The Shepherd Up-To-Date • A Poetic Blacksmith • A Vanishing Trade • From West Yorkshire • A Welsh Village Type • Scottish Village Types • A Danger to Coracle Fishing • The "Little People" • Tricycle Crier

9. Country Childhood 213

A Charming Picture • Punch and Judy Shows • Blind-man's Buff in Many Lands • War Helpers in the Village • Amateur Milkmaids • Starting Well • Too Old for the Navy at Fifteen! • A Reformed Character • A Contrast • Christmas in Shetland • A Tame Lion Cub

10. The Gentleman Abroad 231

A Scene in Palestine • The Bear as a Highwayman • A Titwillow Tragedy • A Belgian Brake • The End of an Ancient Monument • A Punjabi Fisherman • Not Santa Claus • At Hungarian Cross-roads • Safety First in Peru • A Bamboo Bridge

"Just think," she buzzed inconsequently, "my sister in Cambridgeshire has hatched out thirty-three White Orpington chickens in her incubator!"

"What eggs did she put in it?" asked Francesca.

"Oh, some very special strain of White Orpington."

"Then I don't see anything remarkable in the result. If she had put in crocodile's eggs and hatched out White Orpingtons, there might have been something to write to COUNTRY LIFE about."

SAKI, THE UNBEARABLE BASSINGTON, 1912

FOREWORD

One of the particular joys of editing *Country Life* is choosing the letters to be included on the weekly correspondence page of that name. I never know what to expect from the postbag and it is best to expect the unexpected – by the jugful. *Country Life* rarely prints letters of a political nature and this is perhaps why this collection remains so timely, informative and rewarding.

During my editorship, debates have raged over how to poach an egg, the date of the earliest war memorial and schemes for getting fit for the shooting field. There have been pictures sent in for identification, research enquiries from authors preparing books, besides countless charming memories, observations and pieces of advice. The letters arrive from across the globe and they reveal the readers not just as devotees of the magazine, but in-the-field reporters enhancing by their correspondence the institution that *Country Life* has become.

In this volume of letters to the editor from our archives, we look back at some of the most extraordinary correspondence in the magazine's long history. Their richness and diversity are completely enthralling. Many are scarcely believable: would you keep a rhinoceros as a pet; or pursue wasps with scissors; or know how to find a dead rat beneath the floorboards? Others are informative, delightful or eccentric. Some also describe historic events: here, for example, a soldier cheerfully recounts his experiences in the trenches. To a modern reader his account is necessarily suffused with poignancy.

Where necessary, letters were also published with responses from the editor, whose breadth and depth of knowledge seems in retrospect unfathomable. Advice is given to 'a young lady of better society' on how to make a living through riding, moths are prescribed albo-carbon, while one reader gets quite a lecture on allowing her tennis racket gut to dry out. I am not sure how I would answer today the question asked in 1898 on where is the best place to make 'a small headquarters for an idle man', but it is a pleasant thought.

MARK HEDGES

EDITOR OF COUNTRY LIFE
OCTOBER 2012

Country Life

JUNE 28 1941

AGRICULTURE NUMBER

PRICE ONE SHILLING

The men who are fighting the Battle of Food on every farm in the land have their most reliable Ally in the Fordson, Britain's most popular Tractor.

FORD MOTOR COMPANY LIMITED, DAGENHAM, ESSEX

FORDSON
AGRICULTURAL TRACTOR
Completely British Built

LONDON SHOWROOMS, 88, REGENT STREET, W.1

"CAN THE READER ADVISE?"

For its catholic tastes, wide experience and boundless enthusiasm, the readership of Country Life *is impossible to match. Who better to approach, therefore, when all other authorities fail, for information on the arcane, bizarre or curious?*

I

THE OFFICES OF   LON   DON   THE OFFICES OF
"COUNTRY LIFE"   "COUNTRY LIFE"

NOVEMBER 13TH, 1897

DO DOGS SEE GHOSTS?

SIR,—I wish to mention some curious behaviour on the part of a dog of my acquaintance, in the hope that some of your correspondents may be able to assist, by quoting similar cases, in explaining a mystery. The dog in question, a wavy-coated retriever bitch of high pedigree and even higher intelligence, is the property of a friend of mine. She is almost his familiar, and as good a retriever as man need desire to possess; and her favourite resting-place, until recently, had been an armchair in the smoking-room. There, one afternoon, some three weeks ago, she was sleeping quietly, when suddenly she woke in great distress and alarm. Then she jumped from the chair, rushed about in great excitement, and out of the room as soon as possible. Since then she has never willingly entered the smoking-room, and, when induced to go in by persuasion or force, she shows marked signs of uneasiness and anxiety, as I have myself seen quite recently. Out of that room she conducts herself with her accustomed modest dignity. In it she is like a human being that has seen a terror that cannot be forgotten. I have habitually lived among dogs, and cannot recollect a similar case.— CANICULUS

> "IN IT SHE IS LIKE A HUMAN BEING THAT HAS SEEN A TERROR THAT CANNOT BE FORGOTTEN"

DECEMBER 25TH, 1897

FLOATING GOLF BALLS

SIR,—I play a good deal on our inland green, on which there are apt to be frequent pools of water after a shower of rain. I should be very much obliged if anyone can tell me of any golf balls that can be depended on to float. My experience has been that they are just about on the flotation mark. Some will float and some will sink; it seems to be a matter of chance. Surely there ought to be some ball that one can rely on for floating. With apologies for troubling you.—GOLFER

"SOME WILL FLOAT AND SOME WILL SINK"

[We believe that our correspondent will find the "Eureka" ball to answer his purpose in this particular. All those that we have tried seem to have this merit of floating. It is not for every purpose, however, that a ball so specifically light is best.—Ed]

Golf on the Ice, attributed to Wybrand de Geest.
A *Country Life* cover of 1929.

NOVEMBER 14ᵀᴴ, 1941

MILK BOTTLE CAP CUT OPEN BY TITS

Of great interest to ornithologists, this form of "learnt behaviour" on the part of birds was the cause of much comment as it spread across Britain. It is believed that it was first noted by the denizens of Swaythling in Hampshire in the late 1920s.

SIR,—In this suburb, on the edge of Epping Forest, the tits often remove in the early morning the entire flat surface of the metal caps on the bottles of milk left at householders' doors. They do it as neatly as if they had cut out each cap with a knife, and seldom is there even a scrap of metal left lying about. What do the tits do with the pieces? And has anyone ever caught them at their rapid thievery? The bottled milk itself, slightly reduced in level, indicates that, after removing the cap (except for the narrow rim clipping the edge of the bottle), the tits have drunk as far down as they could reach. Whether a bird has ever been caught in the act or not, it can hardly be doubted by anyone who has watched the tit's intelligent acrobatics in a garden that he, and none other, is the clever marauder.—V. H. FRIEDLAENDER, BUCKHURST HILL, ESSEX

[We had not heard of such pranks on the part of tits in connection with metal caps until quite recently, since when several instances have come under our notice. Perhaps our readers can say whether milk-cap perforation is becoming common and when they first observed it.—Ed]

DECEMBER 5TH, 1941

TITS AND MILK BOTTLES

SIR,—I was interested in the letter published in your issue of November 14TH, and in reply to your note at the foot I can say that tits began stealing our milk during midsummer, 1940.

The plan of campaign was to hide in the yew hedge close to the back door and await the arrival of the milkman. Within three minutes of his departure the cap was pierced and the milk drunk down to the level of the extreme reach of the thief with the longest neck. They were always too quick for us, so in desperation we were driven to buy an earthenware bottle-cover which the milkman places over the morning's supply.— G. BARRY P. THOMPSON, HANLEY CASTLE, WORCESTER

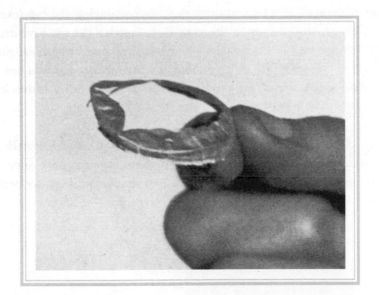

AUGUST 7ᵀᴴ, 1909

FEEDING KINKAJOUS

SIR,—I shall be much obliged if any of your readers can give me some hints as to the treatment of kinkajous, or honey-bears. I have a pair of these little animals, and have kept them in good health since last September on a diet of bananas, apples, white grapes and milk puddings; also dates, jam and honey as treats. I hoped when the summer came to be able to give them more variety of fruit and green food; but they do not seem to care for strawberries and other summer fruits,

> "A DIET OF BANANAS, APPLES, WHITE GRAPES AND MILK PUDDINGS"

and I cannot find any green food that they will eat. I should be glad if anyone else who may have kept animals of this sort would let me know of any other food that they would enjoy. They are very fond of sparrows' eggs, but, of course, I cannot often give them any. They are such sweet little amusing beasts and so tame and pretty that I am very anxious to keep them in good health for the longest period possible; and, as I cannot find anyone else who knows anything about them, I have to gain my own experience as to what suits them.—M. A. SANDERSON

NOVEMBER 23ʳᵈ, 1901

DO DOGS THINK?

SIR,—Some weeks ago a writer in COUNTRY LIFE told how a setter which had never taken water went into a lake to pick up a grouse which had fallen into it. This case of animal reason was quoted in the *St. James's Gazette*, and attracted a good deal of attention, which certainly it deserved. It brought to my mind what I think is an even more remarkable story. When my friend M. Camille Barrère – now French Ambassador at Rome – was French Minister at Munich, he often went out alone snipe-shooting on the banks of the Tsar. He had a valuable retriever, of which he was very fond, and which had never disobeyed his orders. But one winter's day, when the river was frozen over, the dog absolutely refused to go for a bird which had fallen on the ice. M. Barrère was rather angry, and, after urging the dog once or twice, he went on the ice himself to pick up the snipe. Scarcely had he gone a few steps when the ice gave way, and only his presence of mind and the fact that he is an excellent swimmer saved his life. This anecdote shows that animals not only possess reasoning faculties, but that in many respects they are more observing and intelligent than men. I was once told by a student of St. Thomas Aquinas's that the Saint remarks that animals have keener perceptions than men, and supposes that the reason men have not these keen perceptions is that if they had them they would make bad use of them. I should be very glad if anyone would tell me in what part of St. Thomas's writings this passage occurs.—EVELYN MARTINENGO-CESARESCO

> "THE SAINT REMARKS THAT ANIMALS HAVE KEENER PERCEPTIONS THAN MEN"

CIDER AND RHEUMATISM

Country Life *took a keen interest in cider production, and pictures of presses, reports on the cider-apple harvest and anecdotes featured strongly in its early pages. At this time Somerset was not counted among the two premier cider-drinking counties.*

SIR,—Doctors differ – not only with one another, but also with their own dicta. There is at present a notion that if you want to evade rheumatism you must drink cider. The doctors are ordering cider for rheumatism. A few years ago I remember that it was the opinion of the faculty that cider, with its acid properties, was fatal for anyone with a rheumatic tendency. We have changed all that. But what would be interesting to know is whether rheumatism is more or less rampant than elsewhere among the country people who drink cider. The two chief cider-drinking counties, we may take it, are Devonshire and Herefordshire. Now, it is not fair to take Devonshire, with which I am well acquainted, and ask whether the people are more than ordinarily afflicted with rheumatism there, because there are other causes than the cider, namely, the damp climate, that would account for the fact that you see so many of the old folk bent up with rheumatics there. But Herefordshire gives a fair test. It is not a particularly damp, nor particularly dry, climate. Therefore, if some of your kind correspondents could tell me whether the people of that county are subject more or less than the general to the attacks of rheumatism, it would be helpful to me, and a deal more valuable than a doctor's opinion, in regard to which I am afraid unfortunate experience has made me rather a sceptic.—F. J. L.

> "THE TWO CHIEF CIDER-DRINKING COUNTIES, WE MAY TAKE IT, ARE DEVONSHIRE AND HEREFORDSHIRE"

SEPTEMBER 2ND, 1899

SIR,—I had hoped that someone would reply to "F. J. L.'s" letter in your issue of August 12TH as to the alleged cure of rheumatism by drinking cider. My own experience is, after a fair trial, that as far as Herefordshire cider is concerned, no cure need be expected. On the contrary, I found it rather increased the trouble. The reason for this is, I believe, one given me by a London practitioner – that drinking any fermented liquor is certain to increase the liability of anyone of rheumatic tendency to an attack of the complaint.—R. G.

[Good news for the teetotallers; or bad news for the moderate drinkers; which shall it be called? But, since most of us drink fermented liquors every day, the real question is whether cider is worse or better than any other.—Ed]

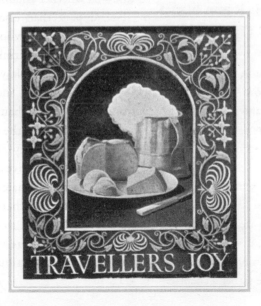

AUGUST 1ˢᵀ, 1903
"A" OR "AN"

Discussions about grammar have also found a place in readers' correspondence. The debate about whether to write "a" or "an" continues today, and there are no end of "puzzled scholars". The modern convention is to favour "an" only before the silent, unaspirated "h", viz. hour, heir, honest and honour, though some authorities allow it before hotel and historian too.

SIR,—Would any of your literary correspondents kindly enlighten me as to when the indefinite article should be "a" and when "an," as I find that many of our best writers not only differ, but have themselves no fixed rule for this question. Some seem to think that because it is correct to use "an" before "h" mute, as in "hour" and "honour," it must also be so before "h" when aspirated; for instance, some will write "a history,"

and in the next page "an historical fact." Now, if it is correct to write "an historical fact," it follows that it would be correct to write about "an hat," "an hunter," "an hen," "an human being," which would be absurd. I am aware that in the "Lady of the Lake" Sir Walter Scott wrote "clattered an hundred hoofs along," but I venture to think he was wrong, and that "a hundred" would sound much better, as well as be more correct. If anyone will try to use the article "an" before a word beginning with an aspirated "h" he will find aspiration difficult, and drop his "h." It seems to me that in all cases when the letter "h" is aspirated, the indefinite article should be "a" and never "an." Again, although the rule is that "an" should be used before words beginning with a vowel, yet there should be an exception when the vowel is "u" long, and pronounced like "you," or "yew," and it should then be "a"; for instance, one would hardly say that an officer wore "an uniform," or that one saw "an yew tree," or hoped for "an union of hearts," yet I certainly read occasionally of "an united family," "an universal rule." When the vowel "u" is short, as in the word "under," then the article should, of course, be "an," as "an undertaker," "an umbrella." Thirdly, can it be right to talk of "such an one"? I certainly find it so written by writers of the highest standing; but as the word "one" is pronounced "won," as in "wonder," surely the article should be "a"; no one would say "what an wonder"! "Such a one" seems to me to be not only more correct, but sounds much better.—Puzzled Scholar

APRIL 6ᵀᴴ, 1907

SHOEING THE GOOSE

SIR,—Can any reader of COUNTRY LIFE explain the quaint old carving from Beverley Minster, Yorkshire, of which I enclose a photograph? The fancy of the old sculptor may, of course, have simply seized on this "droll," to borrow a folklore term, and rendered it in stone, just as fairy tales delight in impossible incident. Or did the artist hail from across the Border, bringing with him the old Scots proverb "Go shoe the geese"? This proverb occurs in the collection published in 1768 by "the late Revd. and Learned J. M. A. Fellow of the Royal Society." The same "Revd. and Learned" author cites a proverbial phrase that seems allied, "You're a pretty fellow to ride a goose a gallop through a dirty lane." Be this as it may, it is a fact that geese are actually shod in Poland. In the Vilna province of Lithuania, a district famous for geese, the birds are driven on foot to distant markets; and to prevent their getting footsore in their 200-mile march to the goose fair held at Warsaw, they are made to tread first in tar, and next through fine sand. Thus the Polish goose fulfils Gay's adjuration:

> "Let firm, well-hammer'd soles protect thy feet
> Thro' freezing snows, and rain, and soaking sleet."

This "shoeing" operation is performed in late autumn. It would be interesting to know whether in our English goose-breeding districts, such at Norfolk and Lincolnshire, where owners often kept stocks of 1,000 birds, any such practice was in vogue. These flocks were once driven to London and other large markets in the autumn, and travelling at the rate of about one mile per hour, would get over nearly ten miles a day. Unless in some way booted like their Polish brethren of the road, we fear the Fenland geese must have spent many a footsore hour on the London highway. Perhaps in the lack of such protection lies the origin of the local cry used by the Lincolnshire drivers of flocks, "Lag 'em, lag 'em." For according to Professor Skeat, the name of "grey lag goose," so commonly used in England, may be derived from the word "lag," i.e., slow, last (thus a clock that is behind time will be called a lag-clock). The word was applied, the Professor suggests, to the domestic species when, settling down in life, they ceased to migrate to Northern haunts, and consequently "lagged" behind their still wild kinsfolk. The Lincolnshire drovers' cry of "lag 'em" certainly suggests lagging and footsore steps. Perhaps some leader from the Fenland may be able to describe what precautions the old drovers took to bring their birds hale and hearty to the London market.—G.

[There are references to shoeing the goose in early English Fen romances.—Ed]

Shoeing the Goose.

OCTOBER 15ᵀᴴ, 1898

BERRIES FORETELLING
A HARD WINTER

The first Country Life *editor, J. E. Vincent, takes a rational line on a common country superstition. Many of his successors were keener to humour the readership.*

SIR,—I think it may interest you to hear that we have in our part of the country this year a very unusual number of berries of all kinds, from the blackberry to the hip and haw and the holly. Now this is always regarded by the country people about us, and I believe with some truth, as a sign of a hard winter in the future. I think it might be interesting if others would tell us if the berries are unusually plentiful in other parts of the country too, and then we should be able to judge more accurately the value of the people's prophecies.—WESSEX

"FROM THE BLACKBERRY TO THE HIP AND HAW AND THE HOLLY"

"WE FIND IT HARD TO CREDIT THAT THEY HAVE THE GIFT OF PROPHECY"

[We are much obliged for our correspondent's letter, but at the same time would say that we have often before noticed in our columns this belief of the country people that many berries foretell a hard winter, but only to express our own dissent from this view. Our opinion is rather that the berries are a sign of the past, not of the future – a sign that the season has been good for their growth. We find it hard to credit that they have the gift of prophecy, though there is apt to be more truth than appears in these current beliefs of the poor people, and it is not impossible that such a summer as unusually favours the growth of berries is often followed by a winter of unusual severity. But, as our correspondent says, we shall see.—Ed]

NOVEMBER 20TH, 1897

SAVAGE AUSTRALIAN BLACK SWAN

Some queries baffled even readers of Country Life. *This one, for example, remained tantalisingly unanswered.*

SIR,—Can anyone tell me what to do with a savage old Australian black swan? I do not want advice of the nature of giving him to my dearest friend, or of giving him a charge of shot. Either of these drastic remedies might be effective, but I want a milder one. I was more or less prepared for the old bird – of course it is the cock – becoming savage in the breeding season, but had understood that usually this fierce mood wore off in a few weeks after the cygnets had left the nest. As it is, the bird is perfectly unapproachable, and is a real danger to any children crossing the park near the lake. A grown man can manage him quite well, if he be fairly dexterous and not afraid of the bird, by catching him by the neck as he comes on, and throwing him off. But even so, one is apt to come in for some very shrewd blows from the bird's wings. To children he is fairly dangerous, and the only remedy I find at present consists in shutting him up in solitary grandeur. One might as well have a stuffed swan as this, however, and I shall be very much obliged if you or any of your readers could tell me of a means of taming him, or of any way of giving him his liberty without his being a public nuisance and danger.—CYGNUS

> "CAN ANYONE TELL ME WHAT TO DO WITH A SAVAGE OLD AUSTRALIAN BLACK SWAN?"

NOVEMBER 17ᵀᴴ, 1923

WHAT HAVE I FOUND?

Sometimes the editor pre-empted the readership with answers of his own.
A native of America, the grey squirrel was released into Britain in 1876.

SIR,—I wonder if any of your readers can identify some curious little animals which are a source of annoyance to gardeners and others near Tring. The country people call them "chinchillas," and say they are a cross between a rat and a grey squirrel. The one I saw had been caught in a trap on a wall, was about 12 ins. long, 6 ins. of which was a bushy tail. The colour was a sort of mottled grey, and the head like that of a rat. They eat nuts, grapes and other garden produce. During the winter they have got into houses and, scrambling about under the roofs, disturbed the inhabitants, and have been found drowned in water tanks and lavatory basins. Some people think they have escaped from some collection or menagerie.—M. C. J.

[A hybrid between the rat and the grey squirrel is unlikely. The animals referred to are probably grey squirrels themselves. They are easily identified by the very beautiful tail with its silvery grey colouring.—Ed]

MARCH 25ᵀᴴ, 1899

TO KEEP OFF TRAMPS

An interesting contrast is evident in the early pages of Country Life: *on the one hand there are many articles, letters and photos dwelling on the poetic and rustic aspects of the "weary Willie fraternity"; on the other, much more hostile responses to vagrants.*

SIR,—I shall be much obliged if any of your readers will kindly give me hints as to the best mode of keeping tramps away from a gentleman's residence by the side of the main road, between two large towns, along which a great number of vagrants travel. The house is just on the outskirts of a small country town, and about 300 yds. off the Union Workhouse. It is separated from the street by a high stone wall, and the back and front are respectively approached through large wooden doors. It is proposed to keep a big dog of the keeper's watch-dog type chained up within view of each approach, also a terrier to run loose about the grounds. Are these the best kinds for the purpose, and what other precautions are recommended?—RUSTIC

> "HINTS AS TO THE BEST MODE OF KEEPING TRAMPS AWAY FROM A GENTLEMAN'S RESIDENCE"

APRIL IST, 1899

TO KEEP OFF TRAMPS

SIR,—Allow me to recommend "Rustic" a simple, but such an effective plan, that I believe if he tries it he will "find immediate relief". He no doubt has some coach roads on his estate, and as these always seem to require rolling, let him politely offer each tramp 6d. an hour to roll them, or give them the same amount for a good hour's digging. This plan has been adopted by a retired general, my next neighbour, and has been used by us both with such excellent results that, although we too are on a main road between two towns, I almost forget what a tramp looks like.—SAFE AT LAST

SIR,—If your correspondent "Rustic" will keep a bloodhound or two able to hunt the "clean boot," he will find (as I have) that tramps lose all interest in him or his. It is more than a remedy – it is a charm.—ARTHUR O. MUDIE

SIR,—"Rustic" asks the best mode of keeping away tramps. I have been told by one who knows, that if you chalk a circle with a round dot in the middle of it on your door or gate, tramps will clear off at once at the sight of it. It is one of their own marks, and means, I suppose, "no good to be got here".—FRANCIS

APRIL 29TH, 1899

GOLD-FISH LOSING COLOUR

SIR,—I should be glad if you or any reader of COUNTRY LIFE could tell me why gold-fish lose their bright colour, and, in the course of a few months after the change has begun, become pale pink – flesh-colour rather better describes the tint. For years we have kept gold-fish and roach in a tank some 7 ft. long by 3 ft. wide and 17 in. deep, and it is only within the last three years that we have noticed the aggravating loss of colour. The tank is situated in one of our conservatories, so the fish are not exposed to sudden and severe changes of temperature; we feed them on various kinds of food, such as boiled rice, semolina, soaked biscuit (unsweetened), small water insects, and occasionally ants' eggs. If you could tell me the reason of the change of colour, and whether we can prevent it or not, I should be extremely obliged.—C. M. MAJOR

[That the fish should change colour after having lived in the tank for several years is strange, but not unprecedented. If the position of the tank were changed it is possible the golden colour might return. Perhaps some of our readers will give us the benefit of their experience.—Ed]

APRIL 15TH, 1899

LIZARDS AS PETS

SIR,—Can you or any reader kindly tell me anything about lizards as pets? Can they be kept in England without artificial heat? What food should be given them, and are they best kept under glass?—A. L.

[Under glass? Yes. Vivaria, as they are called, are sold at any shop where birds, goldfish, etc., are kept. St. Martin's Lane is the great place for these shops, or there are other and, perhaps, cleaner shops further West. The digestion of lizards is very slow, so that they do not need frequent meals; they hibernate in the cold weather, and in winter they scarcely need feeding at all. Flies and insects are their chief food, but if you give them some fresh turf on sunny days, they will find insects in almost sufficient quantities for themselves; but it is kinder to eke this out with some so-called "ants' eggs." Probably any of the European lizards would live in a vivarium in an English house or conservatory without artificial heat. It is best to bring them to England in the summer, when the English sun has some heat, for if brought over as soon as the spring sun has revived them in their native haunts, they are apt to feel the cold, and going back to the state of hibernation seems injurious to them. There are, of course, several species of lizards that have their habitat in England. The great thing they want is sun, so that London is the worst possible place to take them to. Still, they will live there, but it is doubtful whether they enjoy their life. They should always have a piece of dry turf to make holes in to run to when they want shelter.—Ed]

APRIL 29ᵀᴴ, 1899

Sɪʀ,—I have known several lizards intimately which were, and are still, kept as pets by various members of my family. A large South American lizard lived for some time in London, travelled with his master to various parts of England, and never seemed to suffer from the climate, though he had no special cage, and artificial heat beyond the usual heat of the rooms he lived in. Another lizard, who is still alive, and quite a well-known character, was hatched out in England, though of Australian parentage; he is a great traveller, as his mistress takes him with her wherever she goes, and he seems quite hardy, only requiring the protection of a flannel covering to his box when he makes long journeys. Large lizards make most interesting pets, and soon become very tame. Milk and small pieces of meat are their usual food, but I have seen them eat a great variety of things, especially when brought down to be made much of at the dinner table.—V. S. B.

NOVEMBER 5ᵀᴴ, 1898

THE EFFECT OF MUSIC ON DOGS

SIR,—A black Pomeranian I once had afforded me great amusement by his love of music. I had heard dogs howl at the piano, but never before sing to it, as mine did; and what was stranger still, he was always perfectly in tune. This is not exaggeration, but a true fact; and he would go right up the scale without a false note. Whenever I played the piano he used to sit in the middle of the room, put his little nose in the air and join in at "pieces" with a great deal of expression and feeling. He thoroughly enjoyed his musical performance, and seemed immensely pleased with himself. When I left off playing it was evident by his delighted smile and frantic tail-wagging that he was asking me to go on. My object in writing was to say that, from

> "MUSIC AFFECTS DOGS WITH DIFFERENT CHARACTERS – FIERY AS WELL AS MEEK"

this experience I had with my Pomeranian, it is evident that in whatever manner some dogs behave at the sound of music, mine thoroughly appreciated and loved it.

A Welsh terrier we have in the house now often comes and sits close to my feet when I am playing. His nature is a very sentimental one at all times, and meek; other dogs I have noticed do the same thing, and this without either "howling" or "singing." My Pomeranian was anything but good-tempered, meek, or sentimental. At times he went into the most fearful rages when anyone did anything to annoy him. I have never known a dog who took such fiendish hatred to people. With me he was always the sweetest and most affectionate and faithful little companion possible. He was evidently the sort of dog that must attach himself to one person. More extreme opposites could not be found than in him and the Welsh terrier I have mentioned: so it shows that music affects dogs with different characters – fiery as well as meek.—M. F.

26

✣

NOVEMBER 19ᵀᴴ, 1898

SIR,—I have read with some amount of interest your correspondent's amusing account of his musical dog, and, without being able in any way to offer a suggestion, I am emboldened to ask if either you or your readers can explain a similar, and what to me is a most peculiar, feature in the character of a dog belonging to a friend of mine. He is, however, not disturbed when the piano is being played, as is your correspondent's favourite. He does not mind music in any form, but he very strongly objects to the crowing of a certain cock. This might not seem so much out of the way, if it were not for the fact that only when this particular chanticleer raises his voice does the dog commence to howl. The other roosters may crow never so loudly, but they make no impression upon Bouncer, who, as I

"ONLY WHEN THIS PARTICULAR CHANTICLEER RAISES HIS VOICE DOES THE DOG COMMENCE TO HOWL"

say, only joins in making an unearthly chorus when the bird to whom I refer commences to crow. Whether it is that they have musical tastes in common or not, I cannot say; but this I know – those who hear them are strongly of opinion that their voices, like those of many other would-be duettists, do not harmonise, and create very much the same feeling of exasperation as is raised by the musical love-making of the cats in the garden at night-time.—M. L. FORDE

"HAVE YOU SEEN?"

From its first publication in 1897 Country Life *took advantage of new printing technology and carefully selected paper to publish high quality photographs. So important were pictures to the early magazine that it was published for many years under the title* Country Life Illustrated. *As photography grew in popularity, the readership began to send to the editor for publication snapshots of curious events, idyllic rural scenes and even the latest gadgets.*

✢ II ✢

THE OFFICES OF **LONDON** THE OFFICES OF
"COUNTRY LIFE" "COUNTRY LIFE"

SI FRACTUS ILLABATUR ORBIS IMPAVIDUM FERIENT RUINAE

The Latin is from Horace: "Should the whole frame of Nature round him break, / In ruin and confusion hurled".

SIR,—The enclosed photograph of a complete flash of lightning, taken during the storm of July 27TH last, you may deem worth reproducing. The flash went across the sky as shown, above the young lady on the rocks, who seems to be lost in meditation and oblivious of the coming storm.—A. M. HILTON

NOVEMBER 21ˢᵀ, 1941

FIRE-FIGHTING

SIR,—The photograph shows a fire-fighting unit designed by Mr. Keenan of Rock Ferry (and built by his fire party) which would be extremely useful for country districts.

It consists of a trolley upon which is mounted an ordinary 60-gallon oil drum and a permanently fixed stirrup pump, the intake of which is connected with the drum by a short lead. The pump delivery-hose has been extended to 41 ft., and the drum has another 60 ft. of hose for feeding purposes. A double-purpose nozzle completes the delivery-hose, and a stop-cock is fitted to the lead from the drum. The unit also carries scoops, etc.

In action, the operator stands on the trolley just before the drum, which gives him an excellent position well over the pump; which is the best stance for efficient manipulating.

The particular pump mounted is easy of operation – 50 per cent less effort than with an issue pump being estimated.

In working order the unit comes with enough water for 45 mins. of pump action before replenishing is necessary, and the whole assemblage runs so easily that a couple of children can move it fully loaded.

The trolley was made from odd parts, and the total cost of manufacture was about £3 10s.—H. A. ROBINSON

AN INTERESTING RELIC

Antiquarian curiosities have always been a staple of the letters pages.

SIR,—I send you a photograph taken by me of an old cock-pit at Peniarthnchaf, Towyn, Merionethshire. It is interesting as a relic of a bygone and once most popular national sport, and is in a very good state of preservation. It is built of the slaty stone of the county, and has a parapet round the top 2 ft. 3 in. wide, in which holes are drilled for the fixing of benches to view the sport. The diameter of the pit is 11 ft. 6 in., and depth 2 ft. 5 in., while the circumference outside is 51 ft. 6 in. I should like to know if this is the usual size for a private pit, and if there are many now existing. Cocking in this valley was very popular early in the century, and, indeed, within the memory of people now living. Curiously enough, one of its keenest supporters

"THE TERM 'SHOWING THE WHITE FEATHER' ORIGINATED IN COCK-FIGHTING"

in these parts was a blind member of the Peniarth family, an ancestor of Mrs. Scott, the owner of the pit illustrated. An old woman who reared his game fowls for him tells how he knew each bird by feeling it or listening to its particular crow, and that he knew quite as much about the fight as those with full possession of their eyesight. There is no record of any famous mains being fought out here, but doubtless it was the scene of many a contest of local interest. Perhaps it is unknown to some of your readers that the term "showing the white feather" originated in cock-fighting, as game birds with white or light-coloured feathers in wing or tail were proverbially wanting in pluck and given to running away.— CYMRO

AUGUST 13TH, 1910

OLD-TIME DANCING

S<small>IR</small>,—I am enclosing a photograph of performers in a delightful entertainment I have just given in this village. The craze for morris dancing so prevalent in England now has spread to this out-of-the-way Welsh village, and, assisted by the rector and his wife, I have been teaching the school children here for some time past. We helped, with great success, in a church pageant held here in February, and last week gave a performance on our own account. We arranged the stage with a background of trees and woodland, and strewed real hay about it, which was raked into cocks during a preliminary sketch, played by several people dressed as old-fashioned farm labourers and milkmaids, and then the gay little throng danced, and performed their dances with great spirit. The dresses were designed from a print in the

> "A GREAT IMPROVEMENT ON THE MEANINGLESS IDLING ABOUT SO OFTEN TO BE SEEN IN COUNTRY PLACES"

Old Cries of London Series, and were very effective in delicate mauve, green and Indian pink. The children simply delight in the dancing, and since I have been teaching these little folk they have taught their friends and relations, and it is now quite a common sight to see a spirited morris dance going on in the village ground, in a garden, or any convenient spot – a great improvement on the meaningless idling about so often to be seen in country places. I am indebted to Miss May Neal for her excellent books, with the help of which (and a lesson from one of her able young instructors) I have managed to train my little troupe. I find girls and boys equally enthusiastic; and though the boys certainly get a more vigorous swing into the movements, the girls are quite as good in the stick-tapping and more intricate dances.—AUGUSTA COXON, LLANFAIRFECHAN

DECEMBER 22ND, 1923

ST. DISTAFF'S DAY

SIR,—This quaint little etching by Robert Seymour, a good example of the artist's best work in this line, recalls the boisterous mirth of the old-time Christmas. By custom the Christmas festivities properly closed with the revelries of Twelfth Night; but the transition from play to work seems to have been deemed too sudden, and, in rural districts, the so-called St. Distaff's Day formed a *via media* where Mirth and Toil touched hands before the dominion of the one gave place to that of the other. The day, January 7TH, a notable one with our merry ancestors, was dubbed, in jocular spirit, St. Distaff's Day, or Rock Day, because

> "MIRTH AND TOIL TOUCHED HANDS BEFORE THE DOMINION OF THE ONE GAVE PLACE TO THAT OF THE OTHER"

the womenfolk resumed – or were supposed to resume – their spinning. This was done on a "rock" or distaff – the progenitor of the spinning-wheel. The men for their part devoted the morning to preparing their implements, but the work of tilling the soil was not taken seriously until the Monday which followed, known therefrom as Plough Monday. After a few hours of morning labour, a sort of half-holiday was allowed and licence given to play the pranks depicted in our picture. Herrick, in joyous words, gives the popular ritual for the day:

> "Partly worke and partly play
> Ye must on S. Distaff's day:
> From the Plough soone free your teame;
> Then come home and fother them.
> If the Maides a-spinning goe,
> Burne the flax and fire the tow:
> Scorch their plackets [petticoats], but beware

36

That ye singe no maiden-haire.
Bring in pailes of water then,
Let the Maides bewash the men.
Give S. Distaffe all the right,
Then bid Christmas sport good-night;
And next morrow, every one
To his owne vocation."

In the days of which the poet sang, spinning was the occupation of almost all women, and was the resource of the gentle sex of all ranks in their quiet or idle moments. So closely was spinning associated with the sex that in England "spinster" was a recognised legal term for an unmarried woman; and the "spear" side and the "distaff" side were the legal terms used to distinguish the inheritance of male from that of female children. Indeed, the distaff became the synonym for woman herself, and there is an old French proverb that says "The crown of France never falls to the distaff."—A. W. Jarvis

SEPTEMBER 16TH, 1933

IN MEMORY OF THE CHURCH'S HUMBLER SERVANTS

SIR,—Apart from the features of our old parish churches which have their great interest for the architectural expert or student, a church will often be found to contain some object of interest with a wider appeal to sentiment. Such are the helmets and armour suspended, particularly in the later Middle Ages, above the tombs of local families of renown, or the garlands of white gloves which it was a Derbyshire custom to hang up within the church after they had been carried in the funeral procession of a young maiden. The church of Great Bromley, near Colchester, possesses a very rare, if not unique, collection of memorials which may easily escape notice, for they are but dimly seen high up within the tower, above the tall arch which opens into the nave. Scrutiny with field glasses discloses an array of ringers' hats, appropriately arranged just below the ringers' chamber. There are five of these hats in all: two tall hats, two bowlers, and one of soft felt. Two have the initials of those who wore them painted upon them, and three bear the respective dates 1825, 1913 and 1919. One would like to know whether a like custom of commemorating some of the humbler servants of the Church has obtained elsewhere, and certainly these memorials of duty regularly performed have an interest of their own.—E. TYRRELL-GREEN

OCTOBER 26TH, 1907

WASP SCISSORS

St. Dunstan became Archbishop of Canterbury in 961, and is often
represented carrying tongs. This reference below is to the legend that he
caught the Devil by the nose with red-hot tongs and refused to release his
grip until the Prince of Darkness promised to tempt him no longer.

SIR,—I enclose photographs of the wasp scissors made by the Mayfield
Wood-Carving School, which can be obtained from Miss Bell-Irving,
Mayfield, Sussex. I do not know if this implement is a copy of St.
Dunstan's famous tongs or not, but it is equally effective, and spares both
the wasp and its destroyer many qualms. The flat edge of these scissors
fits close against the window pane, one slight nip and the insect is no
more: If used dexterously these scissors do not get foul. I have used a pair
for two seasons in my studio, which is half glass and attracts innumerable
wasps during the late summer, when they seek shelter and crawl about in
a feeble way that is most disconcerting to the unwary. During this length
of time the scissors have not required washing. They are made of oak,
slightly "tooled" and are quite inexpensive.—E. L. TURNER

JUNE 3ʳᵈ, 1899

AN ACCIDENT IN CANADA

This letter is also notable for its confident line on the ever-vexed question of the origin of the term "O.K."

SIR,—Hearing you are interested in all things foreign, I thought you might care to see the enclosed photograph of a railway accident which took place on the O.K. (Orl Kerrect) cutting. The flange of the driving wheel of the engine was broken, and on rounding the corner on to the bridge came off the line; the front bogie wheel on the right side went so near the edge of the bridge as to tear off the 8 in. by 8 in. wooden edge. The driving wheels on the left of the engine broke right through the sleepers, and could be seen sticking through beneath. The O.K. is close to Rossland B.C. No lives were lost. We see COUNTRY LIFE every week and much enjoy it.—M. F. HOPKINS

A WOOL TRAIN IN THE LAKES

SIR,—Wool is the staple product of the Lake District fell dale farms, which are essentially sheep farms, the sheep being mainly mountain-going Herdwicks or Swaledales, the latter being rather smaller than the former. The wool is purchased by buyers' agents who go the round of the remote farms purchasing the "clip" during the end of the summer and autumn months for delivery later on. The valley of Eskdale in Cumberland is fortunate in the possession of a narrow-gauge railway which, though its gauge is only 15 ins. conveys many thousands of passengers yearly, as well as farm goods such as the wool here shown en route for the great woollen centres of Yorkshire.—MARY C. FAIR

MARCH 17TH, 1928

THE EVOLUTION OF THE GOLF BALL

SIR,—At the time when there is much controversy as to the limitation of the golf ball's flight, you may care to publish this, as I hope, interesting photograph showing the ball's development. The balls in the picture are from the collection of Mr. T. Simpson, the well known golf architect, and are mounted on an old lead tray. Beginning from the left, the first is one of the old featheries that were in use till 1848. It has, clearly, had very hard wear.

Next comes the plain gutta-percha ball which was its first rival. This plain ball, in the words of an old golfing poem,

"whirred and fuffed and dooked and shied"

until it was discovered that it flew better after it had been cut with an iron club. Thus we get to No. 3, an admirable specimen of the carefully hand-hammered gutty. No. 4 is the ordinary machine-made gutty, such as we

were familiar with till 1902, when No. 5, the original Haskell, ousted it. The Haskell has, clearly, done good service and lost some of its paint. Very likely, it was one of those for which men willingly paid a sovereign apiece and played with round after round until it was lost or cut to pieces. Lastly comes the modern ball, which flies so far that it is said by its enemies to laugh at the best laid plans of golfing architects.—D.

JUNE 17TH, 1939

CRICKET BATS

One of the true greats of English cricket, Wally Hammond was a prolific pre-war batsman and a master of that most elegant of shots, the late-cut.

SIR,—I thought you would like to see this photograph which shows a Lancashire cricket-bat maker giving the last "finish" to a bat with the aid of a shinbone of a reindeer! Nothing better is known for the purpose, he told me, therefore reindeer bones are imported by his firm in considerable quantities, although each bone lasts a long time.

> "HOW CURIOUS TO THINK THAT THE PERFECTION OF ONE OF HAMMOND'S LATE-CUTS MAY BE DUE, IN PART, TO THE 'CO-OPERATION' OF SO NOBLE AN ANIMAL"

How curious to think that the perfection of one of Hammond's late-cuts may be due, in part, to the "co-operation" of so noble an animal.—NORTHCOUNTRYMAN

JANUARY 29ᵀᴴ, 1910

ATTITUDES OF FOOTBALLERS

SIR,—As evidence of the extraordinary attitudes assumed by footballers in the course of a vigorous game, I am sending herewith some photographs of the League match between Chelsea and Aston Villa last Saturday. What interests me in these photographs is not any point in the game, but the manner in which the camera sees and preserves for us actions which escape the human eye.—X.

MAY 27TH, 1916

A LONDON PET

Sir,—This tame sheep is a regular Londoner, often being seen in the streets of Hornsey on a lead. It waits outside the shops like a dog while its mistress does her marketing, and looks very thriving and happy in spite of what must be rather an artificial mode of existence.—M. DARTON

"THIS TAME SHEEP IS A REGULAR LONDONER"

MARCH 12TH, 1932

HOW AN INVALID
READ THE WIND

SIR,—I send you a photograph of a wind clock on the wall in my hall here near Matlock, which is geared to an ordinary vane on the roof 70 ft. above by a connecting rod and a system of bevel wheels. It was fitted up many years ago for the use of an invalid who was a keen weather forecaster and could not venture out to read the wind in the ordinary way.—T. BEDFORD FRANKLIN

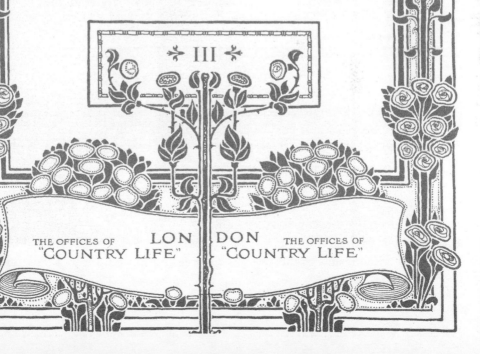

"CAN THE EDITOR ADVISE?"

It has always been expected – even demanded – that the editors of Country Life *display a protean knowledge. The nuances of planning laws, the regulations of the railway networks, the value of furniture, the identity of unknown paintings and the quirks of British fauna all fall within their remit.*

⇒ III ⇐

THE OFFICES OF
"COUNTRY LIFE"

LONDON

THE OFFICES OF
"COUNTRY LIFE"

DECEMBER 10ᵀᴴ, 1898

FOUR-LEGGED GOLF CADDIE

SIR,—I am thinking of educating a large retriever pup to carry golf clubs. There seems no reason why he should not be as useful and intelligent a caddie as many of those bipeds who perform that office for us; and there would be little fear of his speaking on the stroke. The club on whose ground I generally play has a rule against the employment of caddies on Sundays, but I presume that the committee would make no objection

> "I AM THINKING OF EDUCATING A LARGE RETRIEVER PUP TO CARRY GOLF CLUBS"

to the dog's use as a caddie. His conscience, I imagine, is in his own keeping. Nor need there, I think, be any insuperable difficulty about providing a proper harness, in the shape of a brace of panniers, sloped at a convenient angle on either side of the dog's back, in which the clubs might lie, head downwards. So far all has seemed simple, and I have been studying the dog harness used on the Continent for the milk carts, etc., to determine exactly the best arrangement of my proposed caddie's harness.

But then some candid friend has suddenly upset all my plans by assuring me that this beautiful and simple project must all fall through, because forsooth it would be illegal. He does not go so far, I am glad to say, as to maintain that it would be cruel. A big Newfoundland is at least as capable of carrying clubs as many of the tiny boys we now

> "WHETHER YOU OR ANY OF YOUR LEGAL SPOILING READERS COULD KINDLY TELL ME EXACTLY HOW THE LAW DOES STAND IN THIS PARTICULAR"

see staggering round the links under weights too heavy for them. But my friend maintains that there is a law against using a dog as a beast of burden, and that his use in the manner I am proposing would amount to an infringement of it. My present object in bothering you with this letter is to ask you whether you or any of your legal spoiling readers could kindly tell me exactly how the law does stand in this particular. I am, of course, perfectly aware that the law does not permit the use in England of dogs for the purpose of draught. They may not be harnessed and made to draw carriages, cars, or anything of the kind, as they are so frequently used all over the Continent. But would there be anything illegal in their use as I have described? Thanking you in anticipation.—H. G. H.

Over following weeks, the letters pages dealt with queries on sundial inscriptions, Christmas games and keeping down field mice. But this weary golfer's enquiry, alas, remained unanswered.

FEBRUARY 11ᵀᴴ, 1899

A CURIOUS COINCIDENCE

SIR,—I am going to impose upon you for some information which, if you can take the time and will be so good as to give me, will be of very great interest to myself. On page 823 of COUNTRY LIFE, for July 2ᴺᴰ, 1898, there is a full-page picture. The man in the middle of the stream, holding the fishing-rod, appears to be no other than myself, although in this incarnation I have never been in a similar situation. The picture is so exact, being possibly the best photograph I have ever had taken, that I am rather curious to know if it is possible to find out who my double may be; and while it is probably not quite in your line to give such information, yet the incident is curious enough, perhaps, to warrant a little trouble.—JAMES PETTIT (CHICAGO)

[The coincidence referred to by our correspondent is indeed curious. We are causing enquiries to be made as to the identity of the gentleman portrayed in the picture in question.—Ed]

SEPTEMBER 29TH, 1900

HARMFUL SNAKES IN ENGLAND

SIR,—I have lately become a subscriber to your most excellent journal, and I should feel very grateful if you would give me the benefit of your opinion on the following subjects. I have always supposed that there was only one harmful snake to be found in England, viz., the black adder, with the death's-head markings on the skull. Lately, however, I was talking to a friend on the matter, who described a short red snake found in Cornwall and Devon, which is supposed to possess venomous properties. Can you give me any information about this reptile or refer me to any high authority on the subject? I am perfectly familiar with the ordinary harmless grass snake and blind worm, and have seen the adder on two or three occasions, but until recently I never heard of a second nocuous snake in this country. Is there any very great change in colour or marking during their growth, which would lead one to mistake a young specimen of any particular kind of snake for distinct species?—ENQUIRER

[There are two varieties, though not two species, of viper. One has reddish colouring, and the chain of marks on the back is of an angry colour, like the brown on a hornet. The other is more blackish and there is none of the reddish tinge. This is probably the short red snake described as being found in Cornwall. There is a third snake – the Cornella levis *– non-poisonous, in Britain.—Ed]*

MARCH 19ᵀᴴ, 1919

A QUAINT CUSTOM

SIR,—Will you be so kind as to obtain the following information for me? I should like to know if there are other villages in England besides Alfriston (Sussex) where the pretty custom once prevailed of hanging up in the church wreaths previously laid on the coffin of a deceased virgin.—W. R. BULLEN

In response Country Life *pointed out that the custom of hanging "maidens' garlands", or "virgins' crowns" was in fact going strong in the county of Derbyshire, and also in the village of Abbots Ann in Hampshire.*

MARCH 19TH, 1909

AN INTERESTING FREAK

It was indeed a mixed postbag that arrived at the Country Life *offices in Tavistock Street.*

SIR,—The enclosed bird was shot near here, and I am sending it to you, thinking you might know what kind of bird it is. Some friends suggested that it was a canary, but the beak does not resemble that of a canary. The bird was in company with some great tits, and personally I think it belongs to that species, and is a freak of Nature.—E. L. PEARCE, TIVERTON

[Our correspondent made a very good guess. The bird was a great tit, and a wonderful example of luminism. The head, cheek, ear coverts and throat were white, the back and scapulars shading to a darker olive lemon, while the lesser wing coverts and bastard wing were very lightly mottled with black. The primaries and secondaries were white, tinged with black towards the points, the outer web of secondaries lemon yellow, tail feathers and rump white, breast and flanks delicate sulphur yellow, belly a paler shade of yellow, bill, legs and feet pale horn colour.—Ed]

NOVEMBER 15TH, 1902

WHAT IS UNWOMANLINESS?

The editor sometimes misjudged his answers. This sententious response provoked a sharp reaction.

SIR,—A recent writer in your paper on "Harvesting" refers to "hay tossing and such unwomanly occupation." If it is not out of place or too controversial, may one enquire the special need of the epithet "unwomanly," or of the genesis of the curiously unnatural condition of the writer's mind? Could any observer of either sex adduce reasons for the statement that would satisfy an ordinary intelligence? I have had experience of women who were field workers, and I deny that there is anything in any occupation on a farm that necessarily has the least harmful effect. Of course it is evident that this writer looks at women from the standpoint of weaker vessels, morally and physically incapable of being rather superior to their circumstances. He has surely sufficient experience of human nature to be aware that "womanly" virtues are as likely to survive under the coarse habit of the field-worker as beneath silk, and that the heart retains its native depth and purity in rough speech as in those voices low with fashion, not with feeling. A woman will grow as much a woman – perhaps more of a woman – from tending our English fields beneath the skies as in the supposititious refinement of boarding-schools and "at homes."

If women are to have souls, surely they have character sufficient to toss hay, dig potatoes, or fodder cattle. Conventional "womanliness", which is really on a par with "ladylikeness", must give way to the broader virtues of humanity.—FIELD-LOVER

[Our correspondent's ardour is very generous, but trop de sele, madame, trop de sele. Tossing hay is the hardest labour, and woman is the weaker vessel; ergo, it is an unwomanly task.—Ed]

NOVEMBER 22ND, 1902

SIR,—Your postscript with regard to the controversy (on the subject of harvesting or haymaking by women), states that haymaking is the hardest labour. I cannot forbear asking whether you have ever tried it yourself, for I am a woman not born to labour in the field, but delighting in that and gardening, not in the sense of play, but of real hard work. I work in the hay field, apart from the men, and have watched with indignation the lazy way in which they moved their arms, and rested every few minutes on their forks or rakes to talk to each other or drink. I would rather have a few girls to make my hay than a dozen men.

I have got through my raking and making into cocks in half the time the men have taken to do the work. It is not nearly such hard work as scrubbing a floor, or rubbing up plate, or carrying cans of water about. The work unfit for women is lifting heavy weights – I must own that this has tried my strength – but using the arms for such light work as tossing and raking hay is a most healthy exercise. I am sure medical men would say so too. It may be more "womanly" to think of nothing but dressing up and pleasure. We have far too much of that kind of womanliness and frailty, unfortunately, and I am sorry that you should seem to discourage any kind of work for women that has the effect of taking them away from luxurious and degrading influences of the town. We all know that luxury is the cause of the downfall of Empires, and this state of living is found generally in the towns. Of course there are some natures that will always be coarse, whatever refining surroundings they may be in; but education and COUNTRY LIFE together ought to have the best effect on character.— AN "UNWOMANLY" WOMAN

> "WE ALL KNOW THAT LUXURY IS THE CAUSE OF THE DOWNFALL OF EMPIRES"

DECEMBER 6TH, 1902

WHAT IS UNWOMANLINESS?

SIR,—It was a relief to see at least one woman able to defend field work from personal experience, and it is quite accepted among women workers that they have, as a rule, the "heavy end" of farm labour, with inadequate payment.

Men would resent having women stigmatising such-and-such work of theirs as "unmanly," yet they might write of the men who sell half-yards of silk and descant on trimmings in drapers' shops, or select the clothes of their female satellites, or legislate on matters that concern women too nearly for men to be good judges. It is quite true that women indoors have often harder work. A woman who belongs to the fisher class has to carry creels of fish, carry the lines to the boats, on some parts of the coast to gather bait by earliest winter dawn, to bail the lines for four hours, and to wash and bake, knit and mend, for a large family. Why don't men say that it is unwomanly for women who are to live as beasts of burden to marry and bring up daughters to the same labour? But because the idyllic duties of marriage bind her to the service of a man it is all right, and she forms a beautiful part in the equal division of labour in their eyes. The fisherman depends greatly on his wife's co-operation, and it is quite usual to say, "So-and-So can't keep a man yet." Tossing hay or cutting turnips is less of a strain than, impeded by skirts, carrying coals and water upstairs. Let men wear dresses and have to carry trays of heavy dishes up long, crooked, or dark stairs like many poor servants, or work thirty-six hours at a stretch, as was proved lately to be the case with laundry girls, and they would be surprised. Yet these are to be some of the feminine occupations for which fieldwork, with its liberty, health, and purity, has to be exchanged, because the fine moral susceptibilities of men are hurt.—FIELD-LOVER

[Exigencies of space obliged us to cut this letter down by more than half. It were greatly to be desired that our correspondents would try to be brief.—Ed]

AUGUST 26TH, 1916

TO PREVENT MOTHS

SIR,—This year I have been very much pestered by moths in clothes, rugs, skins, and even carpets and beds. Though camphor balls and pepper have been freely used, yet in a few days on turning over again live moths have been found.

Can you tell me the best cure? Even sulphur has been burnt and the room closed for days.

Why this year this pest of destructiveness?—C. S.

[We have found nothing answers so well as albo-carbon hung in wardrobes and the balls laid in drawers. Camphor appears to be no good, and lavender is said to encourage the moths. Old-fashioned housewives used to wrap furs, etc., in linen cloths, which the pests do not like. They also hate tobacco, and an old pipe or two laid among the furs is said to be efficacious where the smell of albo-carbon is disliked.—Ed]

NOVEMBER 5TH, 1898

A DIFFICULT QUESTION

SIR,—Could you inform me through the medium of your paper how a young lady of better Society, with an allowance of £5 a month, could earn her living through riding?—K. K. W.

"CERTAINLY THE OCCUPATION MIGHT BE FOLLOWED BY HER WITHOUT LOSS OF SELF-RESPECT"

["K. K. W." writes from Stuttgart, and is no doubt of foreign birth. We see no reason why she should not obtain a post as teacher of the art of riding to ladies, assuming her knowledge of that art to be adequate; and certainly the occupation might be followed by her without loss of self-respect. If at any time she resides in a well-known hunting country, she might add to her income by trying her hand at hunting journalism; but she would find a good many competitors. Beyond these suggestions we can think of the circus only, but against that there is an old-world prejudice.—Ed]

JULY 9ᵀᴴ, 1898

FROGS BY RAIL

Sɪʀ,—I am about to ask you a question which I hope you will not think it beneath your dignity to answer, or beneath the dignity of insertion in your correspondence columns, in case any of your readers should be able to answer it for me. I am anxious to send some live frogs – not, I may mention, for vivisection purposes – by train or by post. Can you tell me how I can best pack them for a twelve hours' journey? Would it be necessary to give them food for the journey, and would the railway company or the Post Office make any objection to carrying them?—F. L. M.

> "I AM ANXIOUS TO SEND SOME LIVE FROGS BY TRAIN OR BY POST"

[We must admit that we have no special experience with which to help our correspondent in his present difficulty. We cannot conceive any part of England that is not a good deal less than twelve hours by rail from the nearest frog: but perhaps that is not our business. Since "F. L. M." desires to pack frogs, we should recommend a box with damp moss in it. The natural food of the frog is live things – slugs, etc.: but we do not think they would need food for a dozen hours. All these creatures bear fasts with comfort. It is distinctly against the Post Office regulations to send living things by postal machinery. The railway companies would probably make no objections; besides, it would not be necessary to tell them the contents of the box, and the frogs under such circumstances would probably not have the heart to croak. Even stranger things have no doubt been sent by post. We know a naturalist who received, by the hands of the unwitting postman, a box containing several small paper bags, and in each bag several bumblebees. But it was altogether contrary to the postal regulations.—Ed]

DECEMBER 6ᵀᴴ, 1902

OLD BILLIARD RULES

SIR,—I would feel extremely obliged if you would give some information about these old billiard rules of which I enclose a photograph. The table itself stands in an old hall in Essex, and probably was removed to it from some public-house in the neighbourhood. The orders, as will be seen, are exceedingly quaint. The Leader has to place his ball at the Nail. But, frankly speaking, I do not understand how the counting was done, though it is plain that the style of play must have differed radically from ours. To take an example, "He that strikes upon the Adversary's ball and holes himself loses two." Again, "If any person breaks the Stick or

> "'THOSE WHO SWEAR OR CURSE SHALL FORFEIT SIXPENCE TO THE POOR'"

the Mace, he must pay sixpence for the Stick and two shillings for the Mace." Probably my ignorance is greater than that of the average man, but still there must be many equally unacquainted with the mystery of billiards in the days of Georgius Rex – which Georgius I cannot decide. But evidently players in those days were up to as many tricks as Bret Harte's Heathen Chinese. Among those penalised are "He that blows upon the ball when running," "He that strikes the table with his stick," and "He that throws his stick upon the table." However, there is a pleasing simplicity in the method recommended of dealing with those "who smoke (!) or quarrel at billiards"; and I like this, "Those who swear or curse shall forfeit sixpence to the Poor." Most puzzling to me is that table of the odds at billiards – I Love is 54. How interesting it would be if for one short hour of Christmas Eve we could call back the company that used to play in the public-house and listen to their ancient jargon.—A. M.

G · R

O R D E R S

To be OBSERVED at

B I L L I A R D S.

WHEREAS *there is an Act of Parliament prohibiting any Journeymen, Labourers, Apprentices, or Servants, from playing or Gaming at* BILLIARDS, *in any public House, under a Penalty of Forty Shillings on the Occupier of the said House, and* Twenty Shillings *on the Person so playing or gaming : This is therefore to desire that every Person who comes here will give a proper Account of himself to the Owner of this Table ; and also to Caution all those who are disqualified by the aforesaid Act, that they do not game or Play at* BILLIARDS *in this House, as proper Care must be taken to prevent it.*

I. FOR the Lead, put the Ball at one End, and play to be nearest the Cushion next to you.

II. The nearest to the Cushion shall lead, and chuse the Ball, if he pleases.

III. The Leader to place his Ball at the Nail, and not to pass the Middle Pocket ; and if he holes himself, he loses the Lead.

IV. He that follows the Leader must stand within the Corner of the Table, and not place his Ball beyond the Nail.

V. He that plays upon the running Ball, loses one.

VI. He that touches the Ball twice, and moves it, loses one.

VII. He that does not hit his Adversary's Ball, loses one.

VIII. He that touches both Balls, it is deemed a foul Stroke, and if he puts in his Adversary's Ball, he is to have nothing for it ; but if he puts in his own, he loses two.

IX. He that holes both Balls, loses two.

X. He that strikes upon his Adversary's Ball, and holes himself, loses two.

XI. He that plays against the Ball, not striking it, but holes himself, loses three.

XII. He that strikes both Balls over the Table, loses two.

XIII. He that strikes his Ball over the Table, and does not hit his Adversary's Ball, loses three.

XIV He that retains the End of his Adversary's Stick when playing, or endeavours to balk his Stroke, loses one.

XV. He that plays another's Ball without Leave, loses one.

XVI. He that takes up his Ball, or his Adversary's, without Permission, loses one.

XVII. He that stops either Ball, when running, loses one ; and being near the Hole, loses two.

XVIII. He that blows upon the Ball, when running, loses one ; and if near the Hole, loses two.

XIX. He that strikes the Table when the Ball is running, loses one.

XX. He that strikes the Table with the Stick, or plays before his Turn, loses one.

XXI. He that throws the Stick upon the Table, and hits the Ball, loses one.

XXII. If the Ball stands upon the Edge of the Hole, and after being challenged it falls in, it is nothing, but must be put where it was before.

XXIII. If any Person, not being one of the Players, stops a Ball, the Ball must stand in the Place where it was stopp'd.

XXIV He that plays without a Foot upon the Ground, loses one.

XXV. He that leaves the Game before it is ended, loses it.

XXVI. Any Person may change his Stick in Play.

XXVII. If any Person breaks the Stick, or the Mace, he must pay Six-pence for the Stick, and two Shillings for the Mace.

XXVIII. If any Difference arise about false Play, the Master of the House, or he that marks the Game, shall decide it.

XXIX. Those that do not play must stand from the Table, and give Place to the Players.

XXX. If any Person lays any Wager, and does not play, he shall not give Advice to the Players upon the Game.

All Persons who Smoke or Quarrel at BILLIARDS, *or endeavour to disturb the Players, are liable to be expelled the Room by the Majority of the Company then present.*
Those who Swear or Curse shall forfeit Six-pence to the Poor.

ODDS at BILLIARDS.

1 Love is 5:4	2:1 is 5:4	3:2 is 5:4	4:3 is 4:3	5:4 is 5:4	6:5 is 3:2	7:6 is 6:5	8:7 is 7:4	9:8 is 7:6	10:9 is 2:1	11:10 is 6:5
2 Love is 3:1	3:1 is 2:1	4:2 is 8:5	5:3 is 8:5	6:4 is 7:4	7:5 is 7:4	8:6 is 2:1	9:7 is 2:1	10:8 is 3:1	11:9 is 3:1	
3 Love is 7:4	4:1 is 7:4	5:2 is 5:3	6:3 is 2:1	7:4 is 2:1	8:5 is 7:2	9:6 is 5:2	10:7 is 5:2	11:8 is 4:1		
4 Love is 2:1	5:1 is 2:1	6:2 is 5:1	7:3 is 2:1	8:4 is 4:1	9:5 is 4:1	10:6 is 7:1	11:7 is 7:1			
5 Love is 5:2	6:1 is 7:2	7:2 is 7:2	8:3 is 6:1	9:4 is 5:1	10:5 is 10:1	11:6 is 10:1				
6 Love is 4:1	7:1 is 4:2	8:2 is 7:1	9:3 is 7:1	10:4 is 15:1	11:5 is 15:1					
7 Love is 5:1	8:1 is 13:1	9:2 is 10:1	10:3 is 18:1	11:4 is 17:1						
8 Love is 15:1	9:1 is 15:1	10:2 is 22:1	11:3 is 64 1:1							
9 Love is 18:1	10:1 is 26:1	11:2 is 95:1								
10 Love is 36:1	11:1 is 50 1									
11 Love is 67:1										

NOVEMBER 27ᵀᴴ, 1909

LOST GOLF BALL LAW

Country Life boasted extremely strong and extensive golf coverage almost from the outset, and legal quibbles over golfing matters never failed to exercise its readership. The reason for this correspondent's keen interest in the matter is revealed by his particular nom de plume.

SIR,—I believe this is a question which has been discussed before, but it has come up again now in a very acute form at my local club, and I should be really obliged if you could give the proper legal answer to it: To whom do golf balls belong that are driven over the boundary of the course into a private property? What I am told is that the proprietor has a perfect right to forbid anybody's going into his property in order to get the ball. That seems reasonable. But I am also told that the proprietor of the ground may not legally appropriate the golf ball just because it has been driven on to his land, and I must confess that this seems reasonable also, although the outcome of these two seemingly reasonable arguments appears to be that, the golf ball has to lie there, where it was driven, useless to everybody. Thus, by the combination of two reasonable arguments, we are reduced to an absolute absurdity. Someone in the club said that he did not see why the golf ball did not belong to the proprietor on to whose ground it had been driven, but he was at once nonplussed by the reply of another member: "Well, if your hat blew off and went over a hedge into another man's garden, you wouldn't consider – would you – that it was not yours any longer, but his?" This seems to be unanswerable, and to be absolutely a parallel case with that of the errant golf ball. It would be very good of you, and of very much practical interest to many of us, if you could get the law on the point expounded.—WILD DRIVER

[Our correspondent asks a most interesting and difficult question, which some of our legal correspondents may be able to answer.—Ed]

AUGUST 27ᵀᴴ, 1898

DRY GUT IN TENNIS RACKETS

SIR,—"Tennis" wishes to know whether anything can be done to the gut of tennis rackets when the gut is dry. Should it be oiled or not? Also, is it bad for it to keep it out of the press? "Tennis" would be much obliged if the editor would answer this. What an excellent paper COUNTRY LIFE is! "Tennis" has taken it in ever since it was out.

[When the gut of a racket is so far gone that it can be called "too dry," it must surely mean that it has been allowed to get wet and has "perished" as it dried, otherwise the great trouble with the gut is to keep it dry enough. When it gets wet, or moist, it gets slack at once. The great point is to dry it with a cloth after playing in the wet – if it is a necessity to play in wet weather – and to keep it in its press in a dry place. This will keep it constantly taut. Too dry, in the sense of perished, gut might be preserved from further perishing by putting a little oil on it, to prevent the wet getting into the broken fibres, but even this slight moistening would almost certainly have a tendency to make the gut slacker. We cannot, in fine, conceive a too dry condition of the gut that does not imply that it has perished (which is almost always the result of wetting and being left to dry), and for perished gut there is practically no remedy short of restringing. But it is possible to replace a perished string or two without restringing the whole racket. Never leave it out of the press. If the racket really has been left near the fire, or somewhere where it has got virtually cooked, we think leaving it in a normal atmosphere for a day or two would be better than oiling.—Ed]

JANUARY 12TH, 1901

TO FIND A DEAD RAT IN A HOUSE

SIR,—Our house has been overrun lately with a plague of rats. Having exhausted all other known measures to get rid of them, in the absence of a Pied Piper we have had recourse to poison, and now find ourselves living, as it were, on a volcano, in terror of a fearful smell of decaying rat arising from flooring and wainscot. Already there is a suspicion, or the ghost of a suspicion, of a smell. The trouble is that, though we are clear enough about the room in which the smell, or the suspicion of a smell, arises, to locate the spot in the room whence the smell emanates seems to defy all the experts. In the multitude of counsellors, no doubt, there is wisdom, but when one counsellor tells you that following his nose leads him to the smell in one corner of the room, and another counsellor that his nose leads him to the opposite corner, it is

> "CATCH A DOZEN OR MORE BLUEBOTTLES IN A BUTTERFLY NET AND LET THEM FLY IN THE ROOM THAT YOU SUSPECT TO BE THE DEAD RAT'S MAUSOLEUM"

a little hard to know which counsellor is really the wise one. My object in writing to you is to ask whether you happen to know, or can suggest, any means of finding out where the smell comes from – that is, apart from the heroic measure of pulling all the floor boards up? It would be a great boon to all the family if, out of the plenitude of your experience in country house life, you could tell us how we may locate the cause of our trouble. Thanking you in anticipation.—EARNEST ENQUIRER

[We may congratulate "Earnest Enquirer" on the humour with which he faces a situation verging on the tragic. Poisoning always entails a risk of the horrors that our correspondent indicates or fears. If poison be used at all, it should be of the kind that impels the poor creatures, in their torment,

to rush to the nearest drinking-place, thus fairly ensuring that they shall die outside the house. The recognised means of finding out the exact spot where the corpse of a rat lies beneath flooring or in the walls is to make use of more acute olfactory senses than the human ones. Sometimes a terrier will indicate it exactly by scratching over the spot, but you cannot be sure that he will condescend to take interest in a rat that has long been dead, and if it lie anywhere above the wainscot, in the wall, it is hard for him to give you a true guide. The best nose for carrion is possessed by a bluebottle, and the classical recipe is to go to a butcher's shop, to catch a dozen or more bluebottles in a butterfly net, to transfer them to a wide-mouthed bottle, to bring them home and let them fly in the room that you suspect to be the dead rat's mausoleum. After a quarter of an hour or so of aimless buzzing, while they are getting used to their surroundings, they will infallibly begin to settle over the exact spot of floor or wall where the dead rat lies. They are the best of all detectives. Unfortunately just at this wintry season the bluebottle is rather a rara avis, but possibly a few may be found.—Ed]

ON £500 A YEAR!

SIR,—Being a reader of your paper, I am much taken with your plans of houses, and I am asking your advice as to what income I should require to keep an establishment as described below: House, bachelor's establishment, capable of putting up two guests, a small garden for one gardener, two horses and a grass-fed pony, besides a trap-groom in livery. I would like a pleasant country, about two hours from London, where I could get some hunting. I would be glad of any information as to servants, etc., also what subscription to hounds would be necessary. Could I do this on £500 a year when once the thing was started? My wine bill would not be heavy, but, of course, it would be an item in housekeeping. I

suppose two female servants would be necessary. Should I get a decent cottage with stabling, garden, and small field for £40 a year, including rates?—AUSTRALIAN

[We are afraid this is quite out of the question in England. It might possibly be accomplished in Ireland, but in England such a life might be merry – it would certainly be short.—Ed]

SEPTEMBER 10TH, 1898

COUNTRY HEADQUARTERS

SIR,—Can you give me the following information? I am living in England about six or seven months in the year, and wish to make a small headquarters in the best place for an idle man. I am thinking of taking up golf, and perhaps a day a week hunting, but I am not particular as to the latter. What I want is a nice, social district, but not quite a season place. I want more of a residential

> ## "I AM TOLD BOURNEMOUTH IS TOO RELAXING FOR THE SUMMER"

neighbourhood, where I could most likely get introductions and make permanent friends. I am going to try the Royston Herts Links, where I have friends, but I thought I would see other places before making up my mind. Is there any place down South where both golf and hunting could be had, and where people settle? Could one live there, say, up to the end of November? I have thought of Bournemouth, but thought it too much of a season place. Perhaps there might be some place a mile or two away. I am told Bournemouth is too relaxing for the summer, and I am generally away from December to the middle of April. My excuse for giving you so much trouble is that it is so very difficult to settle on a place when one has the whole country to choose from. I am not particular as to the very best links if the district suits. I shall either take a cottage or furnished rooms.—X.

[We hardly venture to answer our correspondent's letter directly, as he desires; and at his request we suppress his name. Our readers may be able to help him.—Ed]

DECEMBER 25TH, 1897

NOISES IN A NEW HOUSE

SIR,—I am the inhabitant of a new house. I am told that in a new house noises are heard far more than in an older one, because of the absence of the dust that ultimately settles between the boards. My object in writing is to ask you if you could kindly suggest a means by which one could prevent the noise – as of people talking – penetrating from the room below to the one above, and vice versa. Of course, one can multiply carpets and felts, one can even, at extremity, have a second flooring made. But is there any recognised plan, such as plugging the interstices of the boards with sawdust, or any equivalent like that for the "dust of ages," that can

"THINKING THAT YOUR PAPER, WHICH DEALS SO LARGELY WITH COUNTRY HOUSES, MAY HAVE SOME EXPERIENCE ON THIS HEAD"

be specially recommended for deadening the sound? Thinking that your paper, which deals so largely with country houses, may have some experience on this head, I write in the hope that you may be able to help me.—DEVONIAN

JULY 25TH, 1903

PHYSICAL DETERIORATION

SIR,—I have read with much interest your article on "Physical Deterioration." To my mind one of the chief reasons for this amongst the poorer classes is the complete absence of fresh air in their houses. Pass through any village or along a terrace of small houses, and look at the windows upstairs – they are tight shut and shrouded with curtains; downstairs the window-sills are crammed with flowering plants, so that it is impossible to open the windows, even if the inhabitants wished to do so. They seem to have a perfect dread of fresh air getting into their houses. I know of more than one case in which an entire family has died, one by one, of consumption, and the windows and doors of their houses were always kept shut, and never a breath of air allowed to enter. Surely, if the vicar of every parish, the doctor, school teacher, and district visitors would undertake to preach the necessity of fresh air and open windows, we should soon have a healthier and stronger physique amongst our working classes.—H. M. APPLEBY

JANUARY 8ᵀᴴ, 1910

FRESH AIR V. DRAUGHTS

Sir,—What is the truth about the antagonism between the Fresh Air theory and draughts? So far as I can see, humanity is divided into two great schools upon the question. One section holds that fresh air should be absolutely excluded from a living-room, every chink and cranny absolutely closed up, and the windows either double or hermetically sealed. The other holds that good health and freedom from colds can only be secured by a current of air passing freely right through the room. When the Fresh Air theorist explains that this current is necessary to clear away the microbes, the other replies that, while he likes his whole body to be in the fresh air, he cannot endure a partial draught which impinges now on his neck or his legs and brings a cold in its train. With which party does the truth lie? The Fresh Air party have this in their favour – that the medical theory on the subject has been absolutely revolutionised of late years. A consumptive patient is nowadays put in bed between a window and an open door, and both are left open even in winter. Yet, when you put this to the Close Air faddist, his reply is merely that he is sorry for the patient, but that he, personally, is not going to take the risk of catching a cold from draughts. Guidance on this matter from some of your readers would much oblige.—Fresh Air

> "HUMANITY IS DIVIDED INTO TWO GREAT SCHOOLS UPON THE QUESTION"

[*We submitted our correspondent's letter to Professor Simpson, who replies as follows: "Your correspondent signing himself 'Fresh Air' asks what is the truth about the antagonism between fresh air and draughts? The antagonism lies not in that fresh air is hurtful, but in a confused idea concerning the relationship of fresh air and draughts. Some people think they cannot have fresh air without a draught, and as experience shows that draughts often cause colds, they erroneously come to the conclusion that they will have none of it. Few can, either in a hot or cold climate, expose themselves directly to a draught without catching cold, and that whether the draught consists of fresh air or foul. The party who contend that a draught is injurious are right, and the party who contend that fresh air is necessary for health, and that occupied unventilated rooms are injurious to health, are also right. The solution lies in getting fresh air without draughts. One can never have too much fresh air provided it is without draught, and just as fresh air cures consumption, so fresh air will prevent people taking consumption. The individual who shuts himself up in a room hermetically sealed re-breathes his own impurities and those of others in the room, and in doing so, renders himself more liable to catch cold when he goes outside to a colder air.—W. J. S."—Ed]*

FEBRUARY 25TH, 1899

MONKEYS AS PETS

Sir,—We are thinking of getting a monkey as a pet, and should be very glad if you could inform us what kind of monkey is most affectionate and intelligent. Are they very subject to consumption? We should keep it in the house, and only let it have a run in the garden occasionally. We should be very much obliged if you could give us a few hints in your paper about feeding and training them, etc.—E. McLaren

[The Capuchin monkeys of South America are far the prettiest and most intelligent. They are procurable from any respectable dealer, Jamrach or Cross for choice. They must be kept in the house in winter. A cage with a good sleeping box is best. They can be allowed to run about indoors when the owner pleases. Feed on rice, pea-flour, scalded bread, carrot, and a little sugar. All this should be thoroughly boiled first. As the Capuchins are largely insect feeders, give also meal-worms and a little minced chicken. Let them catch flies on the window, or caterpillars and beetles when you take them out of doors.—Ed]

MARCH 25ᵀᴴ, 1899

SIR,—I see someone who is thinking of keeping a monkey as a pet asking in your very charming paper which is the best kind to keep. The advice that I, who know something of the matter, would be inclined to give to one and all who are thinking of keeping any kind of monkey as a pet is that which Mr. Punch once gave to persons about to marry – "Don't."— EXPERTO CREDE

DECEMBER 10TH, 1898

MEERKATS

Sɪʀ,—Could you kindly oblige me by informing me as to the South African animal called a meerkat? Where would I be most likely to get one; what does it feed on; and how much would I have to pay for it? I am pretty certain they make good pets, and should very much like to have one. I saw in Cᴏᴜɴᴛʀʏ Lɪғᴇ that you answer correspondents; so I should be very much obliged if you could enlighten me on my questions, whether by private correspondence or in your excellent Cᴏᴜɴᴛʀʏ Lɪғᴇ.—C. J. Mᴜʀʀᴀʏ, Hᴀɪʟᴇʏʙᴜʀʏ Cᴏʟʟᴇɢᴇ

> ## "WE THINK THE MEERKAT WOULD MAKE A POOR PET"

[We think the meerkat would make a poor pet, for it has a very disagreeable smell. The following account comes from a correspondent who resided at Port Elizabeth: – "The meerkats are very common on the open veldt, where they make burrows like rabbit-holes. They are mainly nocturnal, but are often seen sitting at the mouth of their holes; but they are not rodents, and are carnivorous. In size they are like a small domestic cat, but have pointed muzzles and bushy tails. Colour, black and white. Nearly every night they visited the houses near and killed chickens. They have much the same place in the Cape fauna as the opossum in America, and, like the opossum, sham death, and are very difficult to kill. A colonist who catches one in his poultry-yard may break every bone in its body, and leave it for dead; in an hour it will have revived and moved off elsewhere." We presume our correspondent does not refer to the cynictis, a kind of ichneumon, to which the Africanders apply the name meerkat. —Ed]

MARCH 9TH, 1901

A REGIMENTAL PET

SIR,—I hope you will think the enclosed photograph of sufficient interest to insert amongst your "Correspondence." It is that of a South African meerkat, which corresponds somewhat to the Indian mongoose, hence his name, Rikki Tikki. Meerkats are usually very fierce and treacherous, even after being captive a long while, and however young they may be when taken. But Rikki, being born in captivity, was an exception to the rule. He was as tame and playful as a kitten, and used to purr and croon at one's feet to be taken up and stroked. He liked to be taken out for a walk, safely ensconced in one's pocket. The only thing he was afraid of was a large half-bred hound called Pom-pom; and to make him sit up like he is doing in the photograph, I got someone to imitate the bark of a dog by the side of the waggon. This immediately put him on the alert, and he assumed the position that wild meercats do when they scent coming danger. He belonged to the York and Lancaster Regiment, who used to be with me on this hill. Some wag once called him the officers' "Emergency Ration."—G. V. DAVIDSON, CAP'. R.A., WAKKERSTROOM HILL, TRANSVAAL, SOUTH AFRICA

"I CAN RECOMMEND"

It has been wryly observed that the best thing to do with good advice is to pass it on. For better or worse, readers have always been eager to share their knowledge and the fruits of their own experience.

IV

THE OFFICES OF "COUNTRY LIFE"   LONDON   THE OFFICES OF "COUNTRY LIFE"

NOVEMBER 27TH, 1909

THE LAW AND THE BURGLAR

SIR,—If "Country House" will refer to *Stone's Justices' Manual*, forty-eighth edition, 1908, page 813, note G, he will see that he has a perfect right to shoot a burglar. The following is an extract: "As to killing a burglar, see *Stephen's Commentaries*, fourteenth edition, vol. 4, page 40, where it is laid down that: If any person attempts the robbery or murder, or to break open a house in the night-time, and is killed in such attempt, either by the party assaulted or the owner of the house, or the servant attendant upon either, or by any other person present and interposing to prevent mischief, the slayer shall be acquitted and discharged." I have beside me a cutting from a local paper, dated November, 1893, which under

"IT STANDS TO REASON THAT IF A MAN FINDS A BURGLAR IN HIS HOUSE IT WOULD BE FOLLY ON HIS PART TO WAIT FOR THE BURGLAR TO SHOOT OR MAIM HIM"

the heading of "Should Burglars Be Shot?" says, "the *Saturday Review* discusses the theory as to the right or otherwise of householders to shoot persons whom they find occupying their premises, after a felonious breaking and entry, especially at night." Commenting on the decision of a recent case at Manchester, it says, "Mr. Justice Grantham must clearly be enrolled among the followers of the late Mr. Justice Wills, and who could be in a better following? Mr. Justice Wills was asked, 'If I look into my drawing-room and see a burglar packing up the clock, and he cannot see me, what ought I to do?' He replied as nearly as may be, 'My advice to you, which I give as a man, as a lawyer and as an English judge, is as follows: In the supposed circumstances this is what you have a right to do, and I am by no means sure that it is not your duty to do it: Take a double-barrelled gun, carefully load both barrels, and then, without attracting the burglar's attention, aim steadily at his heart and shoot him dead.'" Whether the above is a true record of what the (then) late Mr. Justice Wills said or not I cannot vouch for; it is only a copy of what appeared in the paper, but it stands to reason that if a man finds a burglar in his house it would be folly on his part to wait for the burglar to shoot or maim him without having the first shot.—JUSTICE OF THE PEACE

SEPTEMBER 17ᵀᴴ, 1898

DOG'S DEATH FROM CHICKEN BONE

SIR,—I should like, with your permission, to give greater publicity through the columns of your most excellent paper to a fact which I believe to be familiar, but yet not sufficiently familiar, to as many of your readers as are dog-lovers – the fact that the bones of chickens and other birds are dangerous to their pets. I knew the fact, and believed it in a vague way, but deemed the danger very small. I have had it, however, brought home to me in the most painful way, by the death of a very favourite and valuable dog. Post-mortem examination proved conclusively that a sharp splinter of one of these bones was the cause of death, and I am left to bewail my loss and my folly in not realising the danger in which I was putting my pet when I yielded to his solicitations for a chicken bone.— VERB. SAP.

JUNE 13TH, 1908

MEASURING HEIGHT OF TREES

Sɪʀ,—A simple, though perhaps rough, way of measuring trees is to measure the shadow cast by, say, your walking-stick of 3 ft. and the shadow of the tree, say 80 ft.; then as the shadow of our stick, say 4 ft., is to 3 ft., so is the shadow of the tree, 80 ft., to the height of the tree, i.e., 60 ft.—J. W. H.

FEBRUARY 18TH, 1922

DEW COLLECTING

SIR,—The scientific explanation of dew ponds is that the water acts as a condenser, converts into mist the air above it, and the mist falls as water into the pond. The latter thus gains more from condensation at night than by evaporation in the daytime. This state of affairs is due to the existence of some material of an insulating nature between the clay bed of the pond and the earth, so that the temperature of the latter does not affect the pond. Many people have been attracted by this phenomenon, and now a new application of the same principle has been made by a well known English architect, Mr. S. B. Russell. His scheme consists in reversing a dew pond and making it into a covered reservoir, the cover acting as the insulator and condenser. On a site at Hitchin in Hertfordshire Mr. Russell has converted a small experimental dew reservoir. This has been in operation since the beginning of November, and already a considerable quantity of water is collected in it. A similar reservoir of larger dimensions is shown by the accompanying sketch. In forming these reservoirs a slight excavation is made, the earth removed being banked to form the sides, while the top surface, or condenser, in enclosed by a corrugated iron fence, made more sightly by a hedge around it. The cover is constructed with sufficient slope to allow the condensed water to drain readily into the cistern below, and as the enclosed air is kept at a low temperature, it assists in maintaining a low temperature also in the insulating cover, the condensing qualities of which are thereby increased. Mr. Russell states that his dew reservoirs can be made in standard sizes from 10 yds. to 22 yds. square, increasing in multiples of 2 yds. at a time, with a storage capacity from 12,000 gallons to about 60,000 gallons and costing in ordinary circumstances from £275 to £1,200.—R. R. P.

MARCH 28TH, 1908

COLONIAL INTERCOURSE

Sir,—Among your readers there are probably many "Public School products" and their like – whose preferences are all for the country as distinguished from the town, but who, though they may have some private means, have not enough for a country life in Britain, now that the cost of almost everything which makes such a life worth living has become so great. Anyone in such circumstances is nearly certain to have thought of going to one or other of the Colonies, but, if he does go, is most unlikely to find himself among neighbours with whom he has much in common, except in the towns. If, however,

> "NOW THAT THE COST OF ALMOST EVERYTHING WHICH MAKES A COUNTRY LIFE WORTH LIVING HAS BECOME SO GREAT"

arrangements could be made by which intending colonists of this class could be put into communication with each other before they set out, it ought surely to be possible to start country settlements which would avoid this undoubted drawback. Could not something of the kind be done?—OLD CARTHUSIAN

[Our correspondent's suggestion is well worthy of being considered.—Ed]

NOVEMBER 21ST, 1941

CURE FOR WARTS

SIR,—In the COUNTRY LIFE number of October 24TH, Miss E. M. Delafield makes mention of warts being cured by slugs. She may like to know that my sister was completely cured of warts on her hands when a girl of about fifteen years of age by means of slugs. My parents had taken a small villa at Ghistelles in Belgium, for our summer holidays. There were a number of big slugs to be found in the garden and the Belgian maid rubbed these on my sister's hands. In a week the warts had completely disappeared.

"I AM TOO PATRIOTIC TO BELIEVE THAT ONLY BELGIAN SLUGS POSSESS THIS HEALING QUALITY"

I am too patriotic to believe that only Belgian slugs possess this healing quality.—VAL VIVIAN

AUGUST 23RD, 1919

TO OUTWIT FLIES AND MIDGES

SIR,—As the fly season is near, not to mention the midge, I think that fisher-men and "guns" may care to know of the "Simpsonette," an effectual net patented by Mrs. Simpson. Perhaps I may add that I have no interest whatever in the net, except to disappoint the insects which seek my blood and spoil my temper. The nets can be got at Hardy Brothers', Pall Mall; Army and Navy Stores; and Burberrys, Haymarket. Large numbers have been used abroad during the war.—KNUTSFORD

> ## "TO DISAPPOINT THE INSECTS WHICH SEEK MY BLOOD AND SPOIL MY TEMPER"

[We do not usually publish letters in praise of specific inventions, but so many people are now being tormented as Lord Knutsford describes that we are glad to make this exception.—Ed]

JANUARY 16ᵀᴴ, 1904

SNEEZING

SIR,—In a recent interesting article on deer stalking in COUNTRY LIFE the writer mentioned the fact of having lost a shot at a good stag owing to his inability to restrain a vehement sneeze. I should like to recommend a cure to him, and to all others who find themselves at the crucial moment in a similar dilemma. It is one which I have frequently

"IT IS SO SIMPLE A PROCESS THAT I THOUGHT IT HAD BEEN BETTER KNOWN"

employed when stalking both in the Himalayas and the Highlands, and it has never failed. Briefly it is this: That the bony cartilage, or septum, of the nose should be firmly compressed between the forefinger and thumb, a process which sets up a species of "counter-irritation," and removes the titillation of the nostril. It is so simple a process that I thought it had been better known.—LIEUTENANT-COLONEL

SUGGESTION FOR COLLECTING RAIN WATER

SIR,—The recent drought, unusual at this season of the year, has suggested several novel modes of saving water to country people who have not hitherto been often brought face to face with such necessity, and one that appears to me worthy of some publicity has been brought to my notice lately. It is intended primarily for the saving of rain water for agricultural purposes on farms which would often be benefited by irrigation. It consists in the erection of a great expanse of corrugated iron roofing – say to the extent of half an acre – draining into a reservoir made at some point of the estate from which the water could easily be turned on to lower-lying land. An unsightly erection, it will be said. True, but it is utility, not beauty, that we are considering. And a costly expedient,

it may be added. True again, but when once the outlay has been made there can be no further doubt about getting an adequate water supply. The subsequent expense would be trifling. Moreover, the roofing of corrugated iron would serve other valuable purposes also – as a place for the drying of hay in a wet season; as a storage place for root crops, and so on. It should be noted, too, that it is not necessary to have a tank of such capacity as shall suffice for the whole annual supply of water required, or anything like it. The rainfall is fairly distributed throughout the year, in this country, and it would be enough that the capacity of the tank should be sufficient to insure the tract lying under its irrigation of water enough to make it independent of, say, a three months' drought. This is surely the limit of what we have to fear in this direction in this country.—J. F. RAWNSLEY

SEPTEMBER 5ᵀᴴ, 1925

HAYCUTTING UP TO DATE

SIR,—On my farm (near Sevenoaks) we have obtained such excellent results by substituting a car for horses in the cutting of our hay that your readers may be interested when they realise how simple is the adaptation of car and machine. The advantages we find are that you do the work with safety at about three times the speed you get with a horse. On slopes chains have to be fitted to the back wheels. Adapting is very simple. At one end of a piece of 4 in. timber, iron plates are screwed on top and bottom. The timber is strapped to the luggage carrier by ordinary stout luggage straps. A shorter pole is substituted on the machine, and to the fore end of this is fastened an old gate hinge. A swivel connects the car to the gate hinge by the insertion of two bolts as shown in the photograph. The car we use is a 15.9 h.p. Humber. I adopted the idea from my neighbour, Mr. Campbell of Underriver.—ALEXANDER DUCKHAM

OCTOBER 23ᴿᴰ, 1897

STOOLBALL

Stoolball is still thriving as an organised sport in Kent and Sussex.

SIR,—People are always rather at a loss for a game to amuse their guests at a garden party. Croquet takes too long, lawn-tennis is violent work, and both these games employ but few players. A good game that might be introduced, I think, is the old English game, still preserved and played in parts of Sussex, of "stoolball." It consists of one or two – you can play single wicket or double – boards of ten inches square, fixed at a convenient height on posts, and set (supposing there are two) facing each other at some twenty yards' distance. The bat is the ordinary wooden bat used in bat fives, and the ball is like a tennis – not a lawn-tennis – ball. The bowler bowls underhand at the board, full pitch – so the game has the great advantage that no prepared court or wicket is required – as hard as he likes, provided it be underhand, from a distance of about fifteen yards. The batsman defends the board with the fives bat. The field stands round, as in cricket – the numbers on each side seeming quite arbitrary – and the runs are scored, as in cricket, by the batsmen crossing over, after the ball is hit, before any of the field can throw the ball in and hit the board with it. It is seen that the game is a cross between cricket and baseball, less scientific perhaps than either, and on that very account, and because it is not so rough a game as rounders, excellently adapted to a garden party. Some of the Sussex players are most skilful with the little bat, wielded, of course, with one hand, and hit the ball immense distances. It is an interesting game, as a relic of the past, but also is one that is capable of giving a deal of amusement in the present.—I AM, SIR, YOURS, G. F. L.

ꙮ

OCTOBER 30ᵀᴴ, 1897

Sɪʀ,—Your correspondent, "G. F. L.," in last week's Cᴏᴜɴᴛʀʏ Lɪꜰᴇ, suggests the introduction of the old English and modern Sussex "stoolball," as a means of relieving the tedium of the common or garden party. I should like to say that I have found a modification of golf very popular. It is only the putting part of the game that is called into use, so the area required is not large, especially as all the play is done at one hole. White marks are made, with whitewash preferably, and preferably in the form of concentric circles, having the hole as their centre, at distances of a yard between each, or two yards, if you please – the nearest being at a distance of a yard from the hole – up to fifteen or twenty yards, according to your judgment of the skill of your players. Beginning then with the nearest mark to the hole, you let all the players play in turn until they fail to hole in two. Suppose, for instance, A to commence – or shall we suppose "Tom Morris," instead of an alphabetical nonentity? "Tom Morris," then, we will suppose, holes in two (or less) from one yard, two, three, four, and so on successively, but breaks down at ten yards. "Miss Orr," let us suppose, follows, and continues to hole in two, up to fourteen yards. "Mr. Ball" is next, and is equal with "Tom Morris" at nine yards – all being successfully holed in two up to that mark – and so on. Of course, the player who continues holing in two up to the farthest distance is winner, and if two or more are equal best, they must play off for decision. A very small prize is enough to give much zest to the competition. It is a good trial of skill and nerve, and there is scarcely any lawn so small as not to give adequate scope for its enjoyment.—I ᴀᴍ, Sɪʀ, ʏᴏᴜʀs, Pʜɪʟᴏɢᴏʟꜰ

JUNE 16TH, 1900

REVIVAL OF THE GAME OF QUINTAIN

SIR,—Several times in your paper I have seen observations, with which I cordially agree, on the value that it would be to the country if we could make popular some forms of games that would be useful in teaching the rudiments of warfare. In that connection may I invite the attention of your readers to the description of a revival of the old English equestrian sport of quintain that took place nearly three-quarters of a century ago.

"Viscount and Viscountess Gage," the account runs, "gave a grand fete on Friday, August 3RD, 1827, at their seat at Firle Place, Sussex, to about 160 of the nobility and gentry, at which the ancient game of quintain was revived. The sports commenced by gentlemen riding with light spiked staves at rings and apples, suspended by a string, after which they changed their weapons to stout poles, and attacked the two quintains, which consisted of logs of wood fashioned to resemble the head and body of a man, and set upright on a high bench, on which they were kept by a chain passing through the platform and having a weight suspended to it, so that if the log was not struck full and forcibly the figure resumed its seat. One was also divided in the middle, and the upper part, being fixed on a pivot, turned if not struck in the centre, and requited its assailant by a blow with a staff, to which was suspended a small bag of flour. The prizes for unhorsing this quintain were won by John Slater and Thomas Trebeck, Esquires. The other figure, which did not turn, opposed a lance towards the assailant's face, and the rider was to avoid the lance and unhorse the quintain at the same time. The purses were won by Sheffield Neave, Esq., and the Hon. John Pelham. A third pair of purses were offered for unhorsing the quintain by striking on a coloured bell, which hooped round the waist of the figure, thereby raising the weight, which was considerable, by a much shorter lever than when struck higher up. This was a feat requiring great strength of arm and firmness of seat, and though not fairly won, according to the rules of the game, the curses were ultimately assigned to the very spirited exertions of Messrs. Cayley and Gardiner. Viscountess Gage distributed the prizes to the conquerors."

Such is the account contributed to the Sussex Archaeological collection by Mr. F. H. Arnold. I have ventured to quote this at length, both for its own interest and for the information it gives as to the arrangement of the quintains, etc., that may be of use to any who think of following the suggestions given in your valuable paper.—A. N. C.

Firle Place, Sussex.

JULY 2ND, 1927

"MODERN MAID'S UNIFORM"

SIR,—I have read with great pleasure your clever article on maid's dress, but feel rather "left out," as you give no scheme suitable for the household of a merely moderately well to do professional or middle-class family. Every woman wishes to have her household staff well dressed and in good taste and suitable for the duties they have to perform, but every mistress of a household cannot afford the elaborate uniforms as those described in your paper. Servants would not buy them, and in most middle-class families the mistress could not afford to do so. At the same time I think a pretty and distinctive dress has an attraction for the maids and adds charm to the house. A scheme which is, I think, very attractive is red unfadable casement cloth dresses for the morning, white aprons and Sister Dora caps, and for the afternoon, red dresses in any good wearing material, preferably a nice silky alpaca, pretty muslin aprons and, instead of the cap, which maids really do not like, dark red or black Alsatian bows on the head. Any other coloured dresses look as well, and I have seen brown, green and scarlet, and very well they looked. One should avoid all very pale or faded-looking colours. Caps are essential for the morning and for cooks, as they keep the dust from the hair. For the afternoon a big cap covering the hair is quite unnecessary. Open caps, such as the smart ones worn by Lyons's waitresses, or an Alsatian bow, make quite sufficient finish for afternoon wear, are much better for the girl's hair, and do away with one of the objections to "going into service."—E. M. SPENDER

> "A PRETTY AND DISTINCTIVE DRESS HAS AN ATTRACTION FOR THE MAIDS AND ADDS CHARM TO THE HOUSE"

POSTILLION V. COACHMAN

When Country Life was launched the supremacy of the motor car over the carriage was not yet finally determined. How a carriage might best be controlled, whether from the box or by postillions mounted on the nearside of the pairs of horses pulling a vehicle, was therefore of more than merely academic interest.

SIR,—In looking at some old engravings of carriages, it struck me that the old plan of postillions was so much better than the present way of driving from the box – certainly from the point of view of the people in the carriage, as they must have had so much better a view of the country. The present way limits the view to the wide "stern" view of the family coachman, and the footman, if there is one, also assists in the block. As to looks, how much smarter a

"THE INSCRUTABLE DICTATES OF FASHION HAVE CAUSED IT TO BE ALMOST ENTIRELY ABANDONED"

postillion looks – well turned out, of course. Are postillions now used by any but Royal personages, and what is the reason they have gone out of fashion? Really a drive at some of the seaside places in one of the hired carriages which a boy rides postillion shows one at once the greater view gained. Is it easier for horses to be driven than ridden?

No doubt it is easier for a man to sit still on the box rather than to "bump" along some miles. Any information on this subject will greatly oblige.—SPUR

[We agree with our correspondent that the old style has many advantages, but it is obviously harder on the horse; this and the inscrutable dictates of fashion have caused it to be almost entirely abandoned.—Ed]

APRIL 8TH, 1899

POSTILLION V. COACHMAN

SIR,—Your correspondent, "Spur," on this subject, in your issue of the 18TH March, opens a question of much interest to the lover of the road. I take it that the decadence of ride-driving – as the term is when postillions are used – is entirely due to the advent of railroads, and their consequent shortening of the use of the roads, the kind of conveyance used in posting requiring much care in its equipment. With the present very much improved state of the roads, lighter carriages, and the shorter distances horses are called upon to cover, I can see nothing against the resuscitation of ride-driving, if you except the trouble that one may expect to find in an equipment not in general use, obliging the use of saddles v. reins, and a coach-box. As one who has had much experience of posting, I can testify to the delight afforded by the open prospect in your front as you bowl along in a well-hung carriage, with the knowledge that you have with you all things necessary for bodily comfort carefully packed away in the imperials.

> "I CAN TESTIFY TO THE DELIGHT AFFORDED BY THE OPEN PROSPECT IN YOUR FRONT AS YOU BOWL ALONG IN A WELL-HUNG CARRIAGE"

No doubt the objections are, firstly, fashion, and secondly, the cost and trouble; for, to begin with, your carriage must not have a box-seat. I saw at the Grand Military Steeplechases the other day a posting turn-out in every way admirable, so far as the horses, leathering, and boys were concerned, but the carriage had a box-seat, and so the effect was utterly spoilt. It is a simple matter to have this box-seat detachable, both open and closed carriages, and with this arrangement, I see no hindrance to the resumption of the smart and neglected style of driving by postillions.—H. M.

SIR,—In answer to "Spur," I can inform him that the present Lord Lonsdale, Master of the Quorn, sometimes used, and Sir Walter Gilbey at Elsenham generally uses, a carriage driven by postillions. The latter is a most perfect turn-out, with a fine pair of grey horses, and a barouche with wicker panelling. The whole affair is turned out to perfection, and looks as if it had driven out of an old picture. I remember that in my boyhood the late Lady Mildred Beresford-Hope always had a postillion and two outriders when staying at Bedgebury. She was, as your correspondent will no doubt recollect, the sister of the present Prime Minister. The postillion is not common, but is by no means extinct. I think, however, that there must be few men who possess the art of driving postillion fashion. Retired horse-gunners would make admirable men for this work, as they are splendid drivers. The accuracy and precision with which horses can be driven in this way is marvellous. I recollect sitting on horseback with two officers from the Austrian and Russian armies, and watching the six guns of the Chestnut Battery, then commanded by "Galloping Gambier," go full speed along a path with a canal on one side and a drop of 5 ft. on the other for about three-quarters of a mile. There was just room for the gun wheels, and no more; yet the thing was done, and before we could express our astonishment the battery was in action.—T. F. D.

JUNE 26TH, 1909

SOME DELUSIONS REGARDING OYSTERS

SIR,—It is a common belief, very consoling to those of feeble digestions, that the oyster, when taken into the stomach, executes, by virtue of hepatic diastase, a kind of *felo de se* and digests itself. I recently tried the experiment, and put oysters, whole and masticated, into water, plain, alkaline and acidulated, and found

"I MUST RELUCTANTLY CONDEMN THE OYSTER AS A MOCKERY"

the result nil, except in the case of the acidulated water, when prolonged digestion caused a softening of the liver of the bivalve. Fallacy number two, that raw oysters are always more digestible than when cooked, is not borne out by artificial digestion with pepsine. The oyster stew, being composite in character, is, however, not quite as readily managed by the stomach as raw oysters or those roasted in the shell. Delusion number three, that fermented liquors digest or assist the digestion of the bivalve, was not borne out by the trial; nor was the oft-cited experiment that an oyster dropped into a glass of beer will dissolve found to be correct. As a general conclusion, I must reluctantly condemn the oyster as a mockery; but no doubt the bivalve will still be indulged in by mortals who can afford the luxury.—G.

JANUARY 16ᵀᴴ, 1909

MARKING TRAILS

SIR,—In reference to previous correspondence, I should like to say that the method of marking a trail by tying a knot of grass is practised by the Sioux, the plain Indians of North America. A bunch of grass tied in an upright position as in the first illustration signifies "This is the trail," as tied in the second "Turn to the right" and as tied in the third "Turn to the left." The forest Indians, such as the Milicetes, denote their trail by "blazing" trees. The blaze in the fourth illustration means "This is the trail," that in the fifth "To right," that in the sixth "To left." It would be interesting to know if gipsies also employ this latter method. Stones and smudge fires are other well-known Indian signs.—MALCOLM C. BROAD

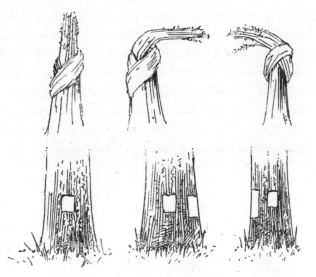

DECEMBER 3RD, 1910

THE VAN COTTAGE

SIR,—I think your readers will be interested in the enclosed photograph of a "van cottage" unit. It is thought to be a solution of the rural housing question, for these reasons: 1. The frame and small iron wheels cost the same as cottage foundations. 2. A timberframed (four-post) building with weather-boards is the most enduring and cheapest construction known, if kept free from damp and creeping ground moisture (such as granaries on mushroom stones). 3. Such a structure meets all building regulations and absurd height of room requirements, being on wheels. 4. At the present moment a rent of 2s. 6d. weekly (which is inclusive) covers over 4s. for a two-unit (11 ft. 6 ins. by 14 ft. 6 ins.) five-roomed cottage. 5. Such a building is absolutely hygienic, and can be moved in whole or part when the demand is shifted from a given locality. It is possible to make pretty thatched roof designs, balcony and oriel windows and so on, and your readers would help on the standardisation and greater cheapness of the labourer's cottage by ordering pretty week-end cottages and demonstrating their great advantages.—BASIL A. SLADE

COUNTRY LIFE
AT WAR

War has shaped modern Britain and the pages of Country Life *offer all sorts of unexpected perspectives on its realities both at home and abroad. Because the magazine rarely reported directly on events – that task was left to the daily newspapers – its coverage takes the modern reader far beyond the familiar concerns and narratives of history books.*

❖ V ❖

THE OFFICES OF   LONDON   THE OFFICES OF
"COUNTRY LIFE"   "COUNTRY LIFE"

JANUARY 6ᵀᴴ, 1900

WOUNDED HORSES IN WAR

SIR,—I am led to believe that considerable misunderstanding still exists on this subject. Animals wounded in warfare are attended to, but only where such attention does not involve danger to human life. It is precisely here, where such attention would, under present conditions, involve such danger, that the bulk of the sufferings of wounded animals exists. It is to obtain for those who might care for them in such positions the same protection as the Geneva Convention provides for those who care for wounded men in like situations that the agitation is being conducted. The letters that have been published from His Royal Highness the Prince of Wales, the War Office, and Professor Holland, as well as private letters received from other distinguished authorities, all sympathising with the object and recommending that steps should be taken to obtain this protection, fully justify the continuance of the movement.—LAURENCE W. PIKE

SEPTEMBER 29ᵀᴴ, 1900

OFTEN WOUNDED

SIR,—I enclose a photograph of an artillery horse which received no less than eighteen wounds as the battle of Colenso. I am glad to say that this gallant veteran is recovering rapidly, and will soon be fit for duty again.—G. NOBLE, NEWCASTLE, NATAL

OCTOBER 10ᵀᴴ, 1914

RUSSIAN PEASANTRY AND WAR

SIR,—I think you will agree that the photograph accompanying this is something more than a picture of soldiers going to the war. It shows the simple, childlike devotion that animates the Russian Peasantry when they gather round the national flag. They have not yet reached the stage at which the cry of culture passes into cant, but they cling to the ancient faith with the pure belief of children and the unquestioning Christian devotion that has inspired so many martyrs and steeled even the weak and timid not to flinch at the pains of martyrdom. They raise aloft the portrait of the Czar, not because they deem him divine, but as the Living Head of that Russia which, with profound truth, has been called Holy. Against a people animated by this spirit the Teuton will rage in vain. They may slay individuals, but the race will overpower them in the end.—V.

NOVEMBER 7TH, 1914

THE RUSSIAN'S PRAYER
FOR HIS HORSE

SIR,—Those readers of COUNTRY LIFE who are so kindly working for the horses at the front in response to Mrs. Arnold-Forster's appeal for wither pads may, I think, be interested to know that the Russians are in the habit of using the following prayer for their horses before going into action:

"And for these also, O Lord, the humble beasts who with us bear the burden and heat of the day, and offer their guileless lives for the well-being of their countries, we supplicate Thy great tenderness of heart, for Thou hast promised to save both man and beast, and great is Thy loving kindness, O Master, Saviour of the world. Lord have mercy."

Those also who, like myself, have travelled over some of the wide spaces of Russia and Siberia, will appreciate the simple trust shown in it, for Russians have often to face dangers alone on horseback in this great country even in times of peace.—II. A'C. PENRUDDOCKE, F.R.G.S.

NOVEMBER 7ᵀᴴ, 1914

"COUNTRY LIFE" AT THE FRONT

SIR,—I think you will be interested in the accompanying extract from a letter received from my son at the front, to whom I send COUNTRY LIFE every week: "I'm devilish glad to get COUNTRY LIFE and sick when it sometimes gets delayed. The only trouble is that it wears out with the rough handling we all give it. It is a comfort to think that there is a COUNTRY LIFE for us to get back to, at least for some of us. The chateaux they have illustrated are fine, but if their photographer were to see some of them as I have, after the Germans have been through them, he would have a job to make such pretty pictures. Think yourselves lucky that the English country houses haven't had the same visitation. I am glad to see that some sport is carrying on. Please go on sending the paper regularly. Even if some numbers are late, they generally turn up two or three at a time."—ETHEL CARTWRIGHT

> "IT IS A COMFORT TO THINK THAT THERE IS A COUNTRY LIFE FOR US TO GET BACK TO, AT LEAST FOR SOME OF US"

[We are glad to publish this cheering note from the front, and will be glad to offer special facilities to those desirous of forwarding Country Life *to their soldier friends.—Ed]*

MAY 15TH, 1915

HOME AGAIN

SIR,—Here is a photo of a soldier home on leave. It shows, at any rate, that, apart from the risks of war, the strenuous, hard life our men are leading now does not seem to affect their health for the worse.—G. C.

DECEMBER 12TH, 1914

LETTERS FROM A SUBALTERN, R.F.A.

A reader of Country Life, *to whom our best thanks are due, allows us to publish the accompanying letters from his son – now serving at the front in the Royal Field Artillery.*

OCTOBER 25TH

We are in action as I write, and every few minutes we loose off a few rounds just to keep the Deutsches from getting *blasé*. There is a battle of sorts going on, but even if I were allowed to tell just what is happening I could not, as I have not the remotest idea.

One hears a terrific amount of noise, and sees absolutely nothing except shells and aeroplanes of all shapes and denominations. I had a somewhat closer view than this the other day, when I was sent with a message to the infantry trenches. There was a lot of firing going on, and we had to cross several places that were being quite plentifully sprinkled with shrapnel – in fact, one might call it quite a "death ride." This is an impression of what I must have looked like if my appearance corresponded with my feelings:

On the way back I stalked a sitting pheasant with my revolver, but he saw my hand shaking, and much warfare having trained him to a high degree in taking cover, he slipped away before I could open fire.

NOVEMBER 8TH

I have just returned from another turn in the trenches. I am going to send you half a pair of field-glasses which have done me a great service. I was standing up in a trench – a little over-confident – watching the result of our shooting through the glasses, when "Biff!" and I received a terrific bang in the eye. Of course it knocked me down, and I wondered for a minute or two why on earth I was still alive. I distinctly heard one of the men say: "Pore devil. 'E's got it in the 'ead." A bullet had hit the lens of the glasses and been deflected by the prism, passing out at the side as you will see. I found half the glasses one side of the trench and half the other; the right half is still quite serviceable, so behold your son with a beautiful black eye. I only wish I could send you the bullet too, but it went the way of all bullets. I am back

with the battery now – rather glad to get rid of a rather nerve-trying job, though it was a great experience and well worth the black eye.

JULY 22ND, 1916

WITHIN SOUND OF THE GUNS

SIR,—A Kentish village church, with the great yews around and the roses rioting over forgotten graves. Within the walls, crowded memories of local knights and squires of long ago. Crusaders in recumbent effigies, and their story marked on crumbling stone and brass. In the porch lists hang the village roll of honour, from manor, rectory and cottage alike, and some names recall

> "OH, IT IS GOOD AT THIS HOUR TO BE AN ENGLISHMAN IN KENT WITHIN SOUND OF THE GUNS"

the family traditions of the old Crusaders. Outside, in the glorious sunshine of a July afternoon, and there one hears, in swaying cadence, yet almost constant flow, the boom of the guns across the sea, marking the struggle still pursued, as in the old crusading days, for liberty and justice. Oh, it is good at this hour to be an Englishman in Kent within sound of the guns.—J. LANDFEAR LUCAS

JUNE 28ᵀᴴ, 1941

A LAMB'S WAR SERVICE

Sɪʀ,—This lamb, escorted by a member of the Women's Land Army, made a good collection in aid of the British Red Cross at Oxford Cattle Market.—L. S.

MAY 24TH, 1941

LADIES AT GREENWICH

SIR,—I have received some photographs which show the work of the W.R.N.S. and may interest some of your readers. I think that it is definitely news that a party of Wrens are now serving in far-off Singapore and, by the by, one of their second officers is Miss Betty Archdale, who captained the English Ladies' Cricket Team which toured New Zealand and Australia during the winter of 1934 and 1935. That she should have helped to take this wartime team east is another instance of the Wren fondness for putting their personnel to do the jobs for which their pre-war life best fitted them.

> "TO TEACH THEM HOW TO COOK FOR 3,000 IS THE MODEST AIM OF THE COURSE"

This picture was taken during the short course on field cookery now included in the Wren nine weeks' training in Cooking for the Navy. The Wrens are taught how to make trenches in which to build a fire, how to prepare the fires so that they draw properly, and to build up the fuel to keep out draughts or to obtain the right amount of draught from what winds or air currents are available. They learn what cooking utensils to use, how to cook the food, how to keep it hot and serve it quickly. The idea behind this is to make them in an emergency able to provide well cooked hot meals for large numbers. To teach them how to cook for 3,000 is the modest aim of the course.—BRENDA E. SPENDER

AUGUST 8TH, 1941

FROM A PRISONER IN GERMANY

*Photographs of prisoner of war camps published in the correspondence
pages were evidently closely scrutinised as readers tried to identify sons,
husbands, and friends who had been lost in action.*

SIR,—I enclose two photographs which I have received from my husband,
Lieut. H. H. Ledger, 51ST Div. Signals, who is a prisoner of war in Oflag
VII C Camp in Germany. I thought that these may be of interest to other
readers if you care to publish them. My husband is on the extreme left of

one photograph (with cap), and the other is a general view of the camp. He says that the sending of these photographs has now been forbidden by the Germans.

Letters are coming through well now, and my husband writes quite cheerfully. He says they are now

"MY HUSBAND WRITES QUITE CHEERFULLY"

playing hockey, and have the use of a small swimming bath. He is also receiving small parcels of food from people in Holland who are unknown to him, and for these he is most grateful.

I have been most interested in reading extracts of other prisoners' letters in your magazine.—JOAN LEDGER

NOVEMBER 28TH, 1941

TURN OUT YOUR PAPER

SIR,—Your admirable admonitions (which let us hope all readers are acting upon) to salvage paper are supported by this photograph, taken the other day, of the President of the Royal Academy. Sir Edwin Lutyens is setting a fine example to us all, but especially to the professions, such as architects, engineers, surveyors, and land agents, that have stacks of filed technical drawings, plans, etc. Many of these must be preserved for future reference; some, no doubt, have legal, technical, or historic value. But a large proportion can be dispensed with, to the benefit of storage accommodation no less than the national effort. No doubt it went against the grain with Sir Edwin to scrap records of great undertakings. But he is doing it, personally sorting out those that must be kept from the bulk that can go to munitions. We must all do likewise and, if necessary, steel our hearts in like manner.—A.R.I.B.A.

"SIR EDWIN LUTYENS IS SETTING A FINE EXAMPLE TO US ALL"

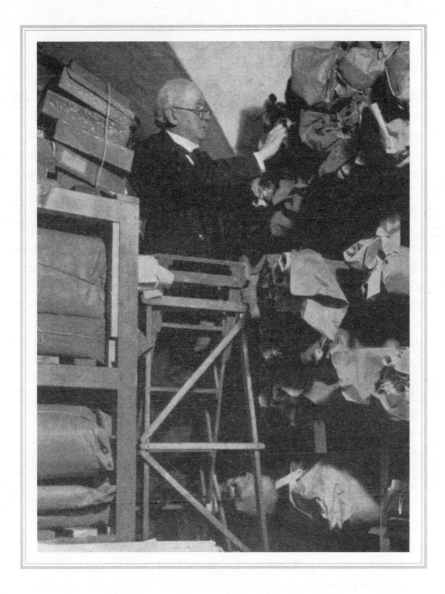

TURN OUT YOUR PAPER

SIR,—My conscience has been stirred and I hope many other readers of COUNTRY LIFE will have suffered a similar disturbance after reading your leading article of Nov. 14.

During the past year I have zealously watched that all wrapping paper, newspapers and other waste was carefully stored and handed over to the collectors, but I have never thought of books, and this is where I came up against my conscience.

I, in common with most other people, like well filled bookcases. I have never, in the past, discarded a reasonably well bound book until I had a new and more desired one to fill its place. Now I have empty spaces, but some 7 cwt. of books have gone to make munitions, and maybe lives will be saved as a consequence.

What were those books? Most of them had no intrinsic value – some had a certain sentimental value, but few would ever have been read or in any way added to the sum of human happiness. Scores of herd books which contained the names of cattle and pigs I have bred, many of which had won prizes and championships at our leading shows; show catalogues with records of past triumphs, bound as permanent mementoes; reference books which were out-of-date; and many novels, travel and other books which never were worth printing, and, when one analyses it, were only furnishing shelves.

As I looked through them the thought occurred to me: "Infinitely better to have empty bookshelves and freedom than the Gestapo yoke which would inevitably control not only our reading but our speech and hearing."

I doubt whether there is one reader of COUNTRY LIFE who could not turn out some books.—THEO. A. STEPHENS, MILL HOUSE, FRENSHAM, SURREY

P.S.—Since writing the above I have decided to go through my bookshelves again, in which case I shall probably turn out another one or two hundredweights, sufficient to make 180 shell-containers or 900 shell-fuse components.

DECEMBER 19TH, 1941

BACK NUMBERS OF "COUNTRY LIFE"

War presents an acute dilemma for the loyal Country Life *subscriber, and a most practical solution from the editor.*

SIR,—I have read your exhortations to save paper, and I am doing what I can to help. But there is one point on which I should welcome your candid advice. I have been a subscriber to your paper for many years, have kept all my copies, and have derived lasting pleasure from them. Do you advise me to dispose of them now?—H. T. FARRAR, FULWOOD, SHEFFIELD

[Other readers have written to us in similar terms. We have recommended them to go through their back numbers carefully, to cut out those articles in which they are particularly interested, to paste them in a scrap book, and to dispose of what is left. In this way they will materially help the war effort without depriving themselves of what they prize most in Country Life. *We would add that our files are always at the disposal of any subscriber who wishes to consult them.—Ed]*

Little Red Riding Hood by JC (perhaps John Constable), 1836.
A *Country Life* cover of 1929.

THE READER'S VOICE

Every reader of Country Life is by natural extension a journalist in the field for the magazine. The readers' letters powerfully convey their concerns, interests and enthusiasms. Also, occasionally, their anger.

✤ VI ✤

THE OFFICES OF "COUNTRY LIFE"   LONDON   THE OFFICES OF "COUNTRY LIFE"

MARCH 24TH, 1923

THE READER RESPONDS

This frank exchange was only published after the event and with the permission of both parties.

AUTHOR TO REVIEWER:

I like your review of my book because it's vigorous and frank. Authors should be grateful to critics who are sufficiently keen on their job to spend candour and energy. You do not like "Desolate Splendour" (and God knows I am the last person to say you should), but you give me generous credit for certain qualities and will therefore not resent it if, after thanking you for this good will, I give you a few counter thwacks. This "bombast" business – Since when is flamboyance forbidden to

> "IT IS AS THOUGH I HAD PAINTED A LANDSCAPE AND THEN BEEN BEATEN FOR NOT DESIGNING A BANK"

the maker of patterns? "Desolate Splendour" is tapestry, and I happen to like my tapestry bright-coloured as well as dim. Further, if I choose to be melodramatic, you must prove that I am badly melodramatic, not that I ought to be something entirely different. "Desolate Splendour" is an attempt to write a tale of terror, a Victorian novel of family and a modern comedy of manners all in one. That the attempt has in places failed I am sadly aware. Belabour me for incompetence as hard as you like; but for goodness' sake leave me the freedom to select character and incident for myself. Is it not begging the whole question of criticism to distinguish between what you personally consider legitimate and illegitimate fictional material?

Do not misunderstand me. I am not claiming for this book of mine any splendour of achievement; I am only trying to justify its aim. When I see myself blamed for misrepresenting modern country society, for

BOOKS OF THE DAY

descending to the level of cheap sensational drama, for wilful defiance of the reader's sensibility, I am shocked and a little perplexed. It is as though I had painted a landscape and then been beaten for not designing a bank. Finally, I am frankly indignant at your accusation of coarseness. That this wretched book, on whose smoothing and polishing I had spent two toilsome years, should be called "coarse" is bitterness indeed.— MICHAEL SADLER

REVIEWER TO AUTHOR:
It is a pleasure to know from your frank, manly and altogether creditable letter that you do see what my intention was. Part of your book is so good that I would place it beside the work of any of those who, in my estimation, are the best novelists. Before I go further, let me apologise for the word "coarse." In my heart of hearts I perceived it a wrong epithet at the moment of writing, but a better word did not come and I was writing with the definite purpose of persuading (or, if you prefer it, bullying) you into leaving "flamboyancy" – if that's the right word – and devoting yourself to the exquisite art exampled in the greater part of your novel. Peacock's feathers are for others to adorn themselves with.—THE REVIEWER

IN A SUBSEQUENT LETTER MR. SADLER WRITES:
For the rest I can only thank you for writing as you have done, and assure you that your sermon, although perhaps subconsciously its contents were known to me for truth, is likely to have the great effect of strengthening a determination to make the successor of "Desolate Splendour" a quiet book, if only my capacity will run to it.

JUNE 28ᵀᴴ, 1924

LAWN TENNIS AT ITS HIGHEST

Sɪʀ,—I am enclosing a photograph of a lawn tennis court on the Gyangtse plain in Tibet which is at an elevation of 14,000 ft., equivalent to the height of Mont Blanc. This is undoubtedly the highest sports place in the world. Further interest is added to the picture by the fact that it is at Gyangtse, the third city of Tibet, and in the background one can see the famous Gyangtse Dzong or Castle, where the Governor of this province lives. At the foot of the castle is the monastery, as well as the town of Gyangtse. As the frontiers of Tibet are closed to foreigners other than to about two British subjects, and the people object to Western innovation of any kind I think you will agree that the picture is particularly interesting.—J. E. Pʀʏᴅᴇ Hᴜɢʜᴇs

MARCH 26TH, 1910

WOMEN AS RAILWAY OFFICIALS

SIR,—While travelling through Brittany I was interested to note the number of women employed on the railway. At nearly all the wayside stations they act as booking-clerks, and in many cases have control of the station as station-mistress. The accompanying photograph depicts a subject which will be familiar to those of your readers who have visited Brittany. It shows one of the women who have charge of the gates at level crossings. They form quite picturesque studies with their Breton costumes, red flags and horns.—W. G. MEREDITH

MAY 21ST, 1932

A RELIC OF A DOOMED LINE

Sir,—It has been announced that the old branch line between Drumburgh and Port Carlisle is to be closed down since there is no prospect of sufficient patronage for it to justify its continuance. I send you a photograph taken in the 'nineties of the old "Dandy" at Port Carlisle. This quaint vehicle, carrying first and second class passengers inside, third class outside, and heavy luggage on the top, was used for years on this branch line as the North British Company's train. In 1913 an ordinary locomotive train was run instead, and the Dandy, because obsolete, is now preserved in the L.N.E.R. Station at Edinburgh.—J. MITCHINSON

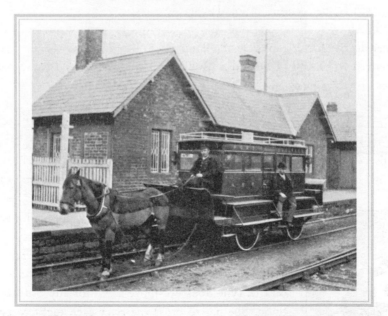

DECEMBER 1ST, 1900

THE PREMONITION OF STORMS BY BIRDS AND ANIMALS

SIR,—If people would only use their eyes and observe the signs of Nature, instead of perhaps looking in their daily paper to see what the weather is going to be, they would be more often correct. A good instance of the sagacity of bird and, still more, of animal life was observed prior to the blizzard and deluge which swept over North Northumberland and part of Durham on Friday, November 16TH, and which has caused more damage round Alnwick than any flood known, also on the river Wear; but in a lesser degree. On Wednesday and Thursday the hedges and woods were observed to be full of rats, also on Thursday flocks of wild geese and ducks passed, making south-east. On Friday the rats were observed to be settling round the farm steadings. About 5 p.m. the deluge began from north-west, and soon came the floods, the river Aln rising 20 ft. Now, the rabbits did not move, though why the rats were wiser I do not know. I observed that the pheasants were very restless Friday, and I twice heard an owl hooting in the fir wood between 10 a.m. and 11 a.m. Foxes appear

> "IF PEOPLE WOULD ONLY USE THEIR EYES AND OBSERVE THE SIGNS OF NATURE, THEY WOULD BE MORE OFTEN CORRECT"

to have an instinctive premonition of floods, as a vixen, whose earth is near the river, always moves her cubs out quite twenty-four hours, or thirty-six hours even, before a big spring flood comes down. A vixen who has her cubs each spring in an island on the Tyne does not move them for any ordinary flood. She has to cross the river each night to get food for them, but as there is always a litter there, we must presume that foxes rather like water.—X. Z.

AUGUST 29TH, 1941

THE LAST BATH CHAIR

SIR,—The war has killed the Bath chair, product of Bath, a relic over a century old. A few years ago there were fifty or sixty licensed wheel-chairs lined up outside the west door of the Abbey ready to take bathers and cure patients back to their hotels.

The last wheel-chairman said in the first year of the war: "My clients have gone as a result of the taking over of the hotels for Civil Servants, and days often pass without a hiring; I cannot continue the job for long."

"THE WAR HAS KILLED THE BATH CHAIR"

These very interesting chairs were handed down from father to son, and some belonged to their great-grandfathers. In the Victorian era there were once 162 available. The invalid, after treatment, had to be kept in the same hot temperature; this could be done only by the bath-chair, virtually an air-tight compartment. It could go anywhere, into the Pump Room, private houses, shops, railway stations, and even into the Abbey for service.

It had been hoped the Corporation would subsidise the occupation as a picturesque feature of Bath life, but alas! it is not to be, even in these days of petrol rationing.—BLADUD

AUGUST 25ᵀᴴ, 1900

AN UNFLEDGED CUCKOO IN AUGUST

SIR,—"In July away he fly" is a well-known saying about the cuckoo, and it is generally accepted as correct, but evidently there are exceptions, as you will see from the enclosed photograph of an unfledged bird, which was taken in August, and as I write he is still swaying to and fro in the reeds, supported by the slight nest of his foster-parents, the sedge-warblers, which structure is just large enough to accommodate his legs, his body overhanging on every side, and when he rises and snaps showing his brilliant orange maw (in true cuckoo fashion). As I put aside the surrounding reeds to obtain a better view, I very much fear he will topple over into the water below, but, fortunately, he settles down again, and before we leave we have the satisfaction of seeing the foster-parents busy feeding him.—J. T. NEWMAN

MAY 31ST, 1924

LONDON SPRING

SIR,—What is, perhaps, the loveliest moment of spring has now arrived in the south of England – and country dwellers are to be envied their enjoyment of it. But to town dwellers, also, spring brings some very charming pictorial effects, especially where the light green of new leaves is seen against the dark background of old houses. The enclosed photograph, taken in Gray's Inn, illustrates one aspect of how beautiful spring can be, even in central London.—WARD MUIR

DECEMBER 23RD, 1899

DOG STEALING

SIR,—I am very glad to see that a determined effort is being made by the police to put down the systematic dog stealing trade that is done in the metropolis. How systematic that trade is will be shown clearly enough by the following instance, which I have every reason to know to be true, and which I think ought to be of interest. After one of the Afghan Wars

"IT THROWS A QUEER LIGHT ON HUMAN NATURE"

an officer of a certain regiment therein engaged had a letter and some papers and a few relics that had belonged to a private in his regiment to give to a man, the brother of the private who had been killed, at an address in a very poor part of the East End of London. He found the place after a little difficulty, and gave the things to the man, who was excessively grateful. Just as he was going to take his leave the man said to him, "Now, you have been very kind to my poor brother, sir. Is there any little dog that you've seen about in London that you've taken a fancy to? I'd be most happy to procure him for you, if you have." I may say that the officer had already told the man that he was leaving London for the country on the following day. It was some little time before the visitor quite comprehended the meaning of the host's generous offer, which amounted to just this – an offer to steal for him any dog in London that he might happen to have taken a fancy to. This story, which I can assure you is perfectly genuine, may serve to throw a light on the ways of the dog-

stealing fraternity of London, to show how little shame they have of their doings, how certain they can make their results: and, moreover, it throws a queer light on human nature in the man's really rather touching anxiety to show his gratitude and make some slight return, and the singular and doubtful shape that he proposed the return should take.—F. L. M.

SEPTEMBER 22ND, 1923

GOLF COURTESY

SIR,—I trust you will allow me, through the medium of your columns, to record my appreciation of an unexpected act of courtesy I recently received from two members of a golf club in the Midlands. I arrived on course, a complete stranger, and sent a caddie to the professional, who was on one of greens, to ask him to give me a game. He replied he was unable to do so, whereupon two players who had overheard the caddie's question immediately told him to tell me that I was welcome to join them at the fifth tee. I am sure I am right in stating that we all three much enjoyed the interesting game that ensued. My regret is that, as the result of considerable experience of other golf clubs, especially in the South of England, I find myself so surprised at the spontaneous friendliness displayed by these two members of a Northern club.—G. SEYMOUR FORT

ʒⱲℯ

OCTOBER 6ᵀᴴ, 1923

SIR,—When the acknowledged Chesterfield of the golf links holds forth on a point of golfing manners one is bound to take even more notice of him than usual; but I confess I cannot quite make out what Mr. G. Seymour Fort is driving at in the letter in your issue of September 22ᴺᴰ under the above title. It seems that Mr Fort recently presented himself at some unnamed golf club which appears, from his description of it, to have been simultaneously in the Midlands and in the North – at any rate, it was not in the South. In his own too modest account of the episode he declares that he arrived on the course a complete stranger; but this can only mean either that he was travelling incognito or that his identity with the Mr. G. Seymour Fort was only fully established when he had himself revealed it. I am not going to insult any golf club, either in the Midlands or in the North, by assuming that his reputation had not reached it. That, however, is a minor point. What happened was that Mr Fort, having announced that he wanted a game, was promptly and spontaneously invited by two members of the club, who had already started their round, to join them. He did so, and the result was an interesting and enjoyable match. In fact, it is clear that Mr. Fort could not have been more handsomely treated had he been of the blood royal. Naturally, he is grateful. Naturally, also, all Southern golfers, contemplating the incident, feel deeply affected by the compliment paid to them in the person of their most joyous representative. But why cannot Mr. Fort be content to leave it at that? Why should he insinuate that the friendly welcome extended to a solitary nomad in the Midlands and the North is something he would be unlikely to encounter in the South? Does he wish us to believe that golf, starting as a game of happy camaraderie in Scotland, has hardened and become churlish and unsociable in its progress southwards? Is it not rather the fact that the hospitable spirit in which he was so memorably received is common to the game wherever it is played?—A SOUTHERN GOLFER

JULY 2ND, 1932

SHOES OF THE GREAT

SIR,—I see the Olympia Horse Show has a new class this year for Grand National winners. I am sending you a photograph of a collection I have of plates and shoes of Grand National winners, which may be of interest just now.—WALTER STONE

[Philippos writes: "The picture of 'plates' or shoes worn by Grand National winners is especially interesting just now because four of the wearers of them – Grakle, Sprig, Shaun Goilin and Shaun Spadah – have been paraded every day at the International Horse Show at Olympia. Manifesto, Jerry M., Sergeant Murphy (killed in a minor race in Scotland), Jack Horner (to the best of my belief) and Covertcoat are dead. Gregalach ran in this year's Grand National. Tipperary Tim's plate is really what is called a 'tip.' A 'tip' is a sort of half plate used in order to correct some formation of the foot and heel. The plates of Jerry M. and Gregalach are clearly from hind feet. Manifesto's plate is not of the aluminium metal used so largely nowadays, especially for flat racers. It is of the old-fashioned iron, and, incidentally, shows some road work."—Ed]

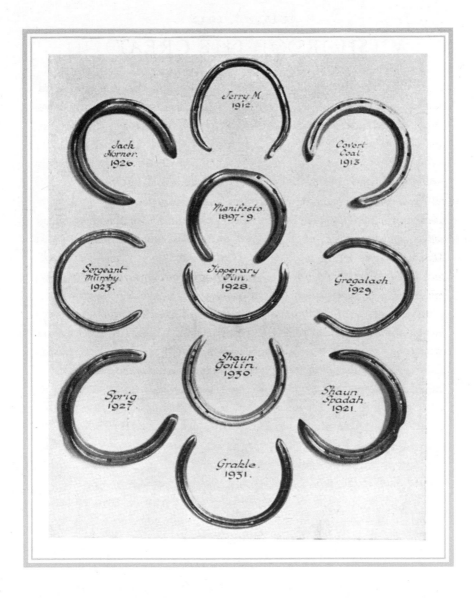

APRIL 19TH, 1941

WILD BIRDS' EGGS FOR FOOD

SIR,—In a note in your issue of April 12TH it is stated that in view of the decrease in the number of fowls' eggs available, seagulls' eggs might well be marketed on a larger scale.

The eggs of the lesser black-backed gulls are regularly eaten by Northumbrian fisher folk at Seahouses and Bamburgh. They are readily available, since the birdwatchers of the Farne Islands take them in view of the predatory dealings of the lesser black-backed gull with the other birds of the Farnes. Those eating them for the first time find them rather flavourless, rather than strong as might have been expected from their fish diet.

The bird sanctuary at Ravenglass in Cumberland is run as a commercial proposition by the Muncaster estate. Beautifully situated on a small creek at the confluence of the Esk, Mite and Irt, Ravenglass has a sandy harbour separating the village from the dunes where the sanctuary inhabited by the largest colony of black-headed gulls in these islands is situated. In the background are Wastdale, Eskdale, Scawfell and the other Cumbrian mountains. The eggs are gathered daily by the watcher and his family and sent to London, the demand having considerably increased since the protection of the plover. It might be noted that the black-headed gull is not a fish feeder, but secures the major part of its diet inland and may often be seen following the plough. Oyster-catchers, ringed plovers and various species of terns also nest at Ravenglass.

In some parts of the country guillemots' eggs are used as an article of food. It would be interesting to know what other sea birds' eggs are known to your readers as suitable for human consumption.—E. J. WILLIAMS

Collecting seagulls' eggs for the Londoner's breakfast.

JULY 12ᵀᴴ, 1941

"COUNTRY LIFE"

Sɪʀ,—Amid the turmoil and anxiety of to-day your paper comes every Thursday to carry our minds back to normality and the peacefulness of the countryside. May nothing ever interrupt the spell of peacetime you bring!

It may interest you to know that my copy goes, after being read by four members of my household, to a lady in Berkshire (widow of an officer who lost his life during this war), then to a lady in Hampshire, whose husband is in the Navy, then to a Naval officer in a south-west town, and then finally to an officer serving on the North West Frontier of India. I occasionally manage to purchase a second copy, which I send on to an officer in the Gold Coast Regiment with other papers.

I am afraid this wide circulation does not help your sales, but it should certainly be of interest to your advertisers!—P. M. Wᴀʟᴋᴇʀ

> "MAY NOTHING EVER INTERRUPT THE SPELL OF PEACETIME YOU BRING!"

JULY 1ˢᵀ, 1899

HAY FEVER

SIR,—My earliest recollections of hay fever are connected with Harrow. June was to me there a month of uninterrupted misery. Life was a ceaseless weep, an almost ceaseless sneeze, and the weeping and sneezing seemed, if possible, worse on Sundays in the hayfields than on other days elsewhere. Proximity to hayfields seemed to accentuate it, so, boy-like, I

unreflectingly suppose that hay was the *fons et origo mali.* In later years I have seen reason to modify that opinion. I was in the Harrow XI, and in the hay fever season I was not infrequently transferred to long-leg, a post now, I believe, absolutely obsolete. My eyes were blurred with tears, so that I could not see clearly enough to field quickly near the wicket, whereas by squeezing my eyelids lightly together whenever the batsman hit to leg, I could see for a moment clearly enough to field a ball when it had to travel several tens of yards from the bat. From this physical defect, which was, fortunately, only temporary, I obtained the sobriquet of "Blink Bonny," after a well-known race-horse of the period.

The premonitory symptom of hay fever is a slight itching of the eyelids, usually combined with some little discomfort in the fauces. Day by day the irritation in throat and eyes increases. You feel impelled to rub your eyes, and to contract the back of your mouth near the uvula, so as to rub the two surfaces, upper and lower, together. The itching seems gradually to extend to the internal membranes of the ears. Sneezing begins, at first in isolated attacks, perhaps only one or two sneezes at a time. Soon the attacks increase in frequency and intensity, till in a single paroxysm you may sneeze violently forty or fifty times: and when the attack of sneezing comes to an end you feel quite dazed and giddy, and probably have a racking headache from the incessant shocks to the brain.

The throat irritation extends gradually to the casing of the lungs, and in very bad attacks you feel as if you were itching internally from shoulder to shoulder, especially at the points of the lungs...

[Our correspondent here gives a description of hay fever worthy of Poe himself.]

I have much more to say about the subject, especially little bits of advice about palliatives to the afflicted. But "lovely June" already holds us in her embrace, so I close this letter with repetition of the simple advice, "Keep yourselves warm – even uncomfortably warm – with woollen under-clothing, fitting moderately close to the body."—BLINK BONNY

[It is with sincere regret that we have been compelled to eliminate parts of this very interesting letter.—Ed]

JANUARY 11ᵀᴴ, 1941

THE FIRST SNOWDROP

SIR,—On December 29ᵀᴴ the first snowdrop opened here, and is now hidden in snow. The date is early, the earliest I have known, and readers of COUNTRY LIFE may be interested in comparing this flowering date, along the seaboard of the far north-western Highlands, with the first snowdrop dates in England.—SETON GORDON, ISLE OF SKYE

JULY 6ᵀᴴ, 1907

VOYAGES ON SOME SCOTCH RIVERS

SIR,—I notice in your issue of June 1ˢᵀ that Mr. Bertram Smith claims to be the one man in 1,000 years to have navigated some of the Scotch rivers. This may be so in some cases, but as regards the Tweed it is not correct, for when a member of the York Amateur Rowing Club in 1876 I paddled my own canoe from a mile above Kelso Bridge to the sea. During the voyage I was frequently told it was the first canoe seen on the river.—ALEC CHRISTENSON

> "I PADDLED MY OWN CANOE FROM A MILE ABOVE KELSO BRIDGE TO THE SEA"

SEPTEMBER 3RD, 1898

FROGS AS WEATHER INDICATORS

SIR,—I see a paragraph in your "Country Notes" on the subject of the colour of a frog giving indication of approaching changes in weather – as the country people believe. I cannot say anything about our own English frogs; but this I know very well, that both in cages and in a state of Nature the little green tree frogs that one finds in the South of France and so on change colour very much with the impending changes of weather, so much so that they act as a very faithful barometer. When the weather is going to rain – by

> "THE COLOUR OF A FROG GIVING INDICATION OF APPROACHING CHANGES IN WEATHER"

which I mean, I suppose, when there is moisture in the atmosphere – these little fellows are of a brilliant green. When the air is very dry they get very dull and miserable-looking. The effect is as obvious in captivity in England as in their wild state abroad. They make most amusing little pets, fly-catching, and stroking their throats in the most amusingly appreciative way as the fly goes down. I infer, therefore, that, as in the case of most of our country people's beliefs, there is a basis of fact in this theory of theirs about the barometric change of colour of our own frogs.—AJAX

MARCH 9TH, 1907

OLD FIELD NAMES

SIR,—I have been greatly interested in the letters on this subject which have lately appeared in COUNTRY LIFE.

The names so far given have been from the Southern and Eastern Counties, but in the North we have many quite as remarkable, and whose etymology is often quite as puzzling. The following occur in Northumberland. To some of them I append possible solutions; perhaps some of your readers may be able to suggest better ones. Syke, or letch, a hollow, generally a marshy one. Warsail Latch long puzzled me; but is, I believe, only a corruption of square sail letch, a name given to the field (near the coast) from its supposed resemblance in shape to the sail, which gradually came to be pronounced quar sail, and now warsall. Other fields with similar names are not uncommon, as Main Sail and Long Sheet. Pity Syke is merely peaty bog; and Velvet Close has been supposed to be well wet close, though as to this there may be room for doubt, v and w not being interchangeable in the North as they are in some places, unless it be suggested that a farmer of German descent first gave the field its name. Prashy Syke is probably an euphonism of rushy syke. Yarelaw (and, perhaps, Warelaw), Yarley Knowe and Yarrell are, I believe, nothing more than guard law, or yard hill, and therefore synonymous with watch law, of which there are so many on both sides of the Border. The same derivation gives us Yearle, Errill and Earl. Lukinarks is a curious name, which, it has been supposed, may be from lucken, in Border Scotch, a bog,

and Airig, in Gaelic, a summer pasture. Swettercroft may be simply sweeter; but what of Switcher Down and Alley Strother? A field now rejoicing in the name of Farthing Piece has, I believe, no connection with our smallest common currency, but is the far ane, in reference to its distance from the steading.

It changed into farthing when the name had to be committed to paper, perhaps by the village schoolmaster, or some other stickler for good English spelling! Goosey Close may have reference to the bird, but may, on the other hand, have the same derivation as Gosforth, which signifies the ford over the Ouse, and hence means oozy close.

Acheron Hill is probably only Acorn Hill, in reference to a former oak wood there. Elyhaugh, Elyshaw, and similar names may have been bestowed from eels found about the

> "IT CHANGED WHEN THE NAME HAD TO BE COMMITTED TO PAPER, PERHAPS BY THE VILLAGE SCHOOLMASTER, OR SOME OTHER STICKLER FOR GOOD ENGLISH SPELLING!"

fields, after dewy or wet nights – when these fish are well known to quit the water – and make considerable excursions upon land. There is a tradition of "The lang gaunts o' Elishaw" (a hamlet on the banks of the river Rede) which were looked upon as a species of ghoul which, in the form of serpents, roamed over the meadows at night to feast upon the bodies of the slain brought down by the stream from the scene of some border fray.—L. G.

MAY 5TH, 1906

THE PADSTOW HOBBY-HORSE DANCE

SIR,—The Padstow Hobby-horse Dance is a grotesque custom of very great antiquity, and there is nothing but tradition upon which its origin may be founded. From time immemorial the custom has been celebrated in Padstow on May 1ST of each year. At 10 a.m. the hobby-horse makes its appearance with singing and dancing, to the great delight of its followers of both sexes. The man who figures as the hobby-horse is dressed in a savage-looking mask, resembling a fantastic horse with flowing plume and tail; an enormous hoop encircles the waist, supporting a tarpaulin drapery which reaches to the ground, and he is led by a dancing masked guide and attendants with musical instruments, the most prominent of which is a drum. So he goes about the town accompanied by a vast crowd of maids in white dresses decorated with flowers, singing May songs, and merry men firing powder shots from pistols. These old May games were at one time universal throughout the British Isles, but appear to have gradually died out; Padstow is probably the only place where this quaint May Day custom is carried on. Sir Walter Scott refers to it in "The Abbot," where he says: "One fellow with a horse-head painted before him, and a tail behind, and the whole covered with a long foot-cloth, ambled, carolled, pranced, and plunged as he performed the celebrated part of the Hobby-horse." The custom is absurdly grotesque, but is an interesting remnant of the merry Elizabethan days.—A. B.

FEBRUARY 18TH, 1939

YORKSHIRE SWORD DANCERS

SIR,—Two hundred or so years ago several villages in Yorkshire possessed teams of sword dancers, but to-day only one team remains, the Goathland Plough Stots or Yorkshire Long Sword Dancers. These, too, had died out, but happily were revived about fifteen years ago through the enterprise of Mr. F. W. Dowson of New Wath, Goathland, a keen student of the Yorkshire dialect.

Commencing their activities on Plough Monday, they tour the various towns and villages in the vicinity, performing various picturesque evolutions, but specialising in the Yorkshire Long Sword Dance, which dance finishes with one of their number holding aloft the intertwined swords of all the performers, while the whole of them circle around.

Clad in grotesque costumes and bedecked with many ribbons, they are always a source of considerable interest, and their annual visitations are eagerly anticipated. When performing near home a plough is part of their equipment, and this, drawn by two of their members, can possibly explain the meaning of the word "slot" – i.e., bullock, which years ago were the beasts used for ploughing.

> "WOE BETIDE THE UNFORTUNATE HOUSEHOLDER WHO REFUSED A DONATION TO THE FUNDS"

The team is drawn entirely from village lads, and in order to perpetuate the custom Mr. Dowson is arranging to train local schoolchildren, in order that they may take their places in the team in future years. A fiddler provides the music.

In years gone by, when discipline was not so severe, woe betide the unfortunate householder who refused a donation to the funds; he often found the forecourt of his house turned over by the plough. This latter implement is not often taken far afield nowadays. They are, moreover, now a very law-abiding company.—J. F. SEAMAN

SEPTEMBER 13TH, 1919

BARLOW WELL DRESSING

SIR,—An old custom of dressing the wells has just been carried out at Barlow village in Derbyshire. It is many years since the great drought in Derbyshire, when crowds flocked to the well which never failed in its water supply. How grateful they must have felt to the well which had a continual supply, when their own wells had long since failed. In honour of the occasion they decorated it with flowers and evergreens. It is now between thirty and forty years since the well was first dressed, and it has long been dry, probably through coal workings, which have drained away the supply. The dressing is done as follows: A lattice framework is first made and covered with clay. The design is then drawn on paper and placed on the clay, cut out and then filled in with larch bark. The paper is then taken off and the design worked in with moss, parsley

and flowers. The design represents Major Wilson's Barlow Hounds, and is arranged in four panels, showing, "The Meet," with hounds and huntsmen assembled; "Tally Ho!" gives a view of the fox, with dogs and huntsmen; "Full Cry," shows the hunt; and "The Kill," depicts the capture of the fox. An archway over is worked in flowers and bears the words, "Peace and Goodwill to All Men," and surmounting the whole is a horse's head. The flowers used in making the picture are rambler roses, stocks, chrysanthemums, yarrow, and others, together with parsley and black and silver moss. On completion of the dressing the ceremony of blessing the well is performed by the Vicar of the village.—CHAS. BAKER

JULY 2ND, 1904

THE CUCKOO'S TUNE

SIR,—Some of your readers may be interested in hearing of a cuckoo who haunted the neighbourhood of a country house in Berkshire for five seasons consecutively, and from April to June never "changed his tune," which consisted of three clear notes, not "a stammer." I have heard his cry at nearly all hours of the night and day with no variation. His return each spring was noted with interest. The village children called him "the cuckoo that hollers double!" (N.B. Even nightingales holler in Berks!) In the fifth year it was observed that the voice of "our cuckoo" was weak and hoarse and he was never heard again!—E. H. S.

JULY 6TH, 1901

BOGGARTS, FAIRIES, AND RUNNING WATER

When horses shied or took fright, it was often attributed to their having seen a "boggart". Thanks to the huge success of the Harry Potter books and films, this old English name for a malevolent spirit is now once again well known.

SIR,—I see in Mr. Cornish's very pleasant article on single-span bridges, that he mentions the idea that the Devonshire "boggart," or bogey, cannot cross running water, and that the children, when out after dark, dash over a bridge to be safely away from him. May I supplement this with a very pretty fancy that the Highlanders have in Skye, and probably on the mainland too, that the "fairies" – equivalent in small malevolence to the Devonian Boggart – are "very bad" – this is the way they speak of them, rather as if they were speaking of midges – at the running water, and that it is not safe for anyone that is grown up to go down to the running water, nor, above all, to cross it after dark? But, they say, the fairies will not touch a little child nor anyone that is with a little child. And I may mention that once, when I was staying in Skye, a tailor came from the neighbouring crofter township to do some jobs in the house. As night fell, he was anxious to go home, though his work was almost done, but he explained that he had to cross running water on his way home, so could not be out, on account of the fairies, after nightfall. He must go at once. We persuaded him, however, to stay and finish his work by getting the inn keeper's little girl from over the road to walk home with him across the running water (we had already offered to accompany him, as a posse, with guns, but had been rejected as quite inefficacious). It is a pretty fancy, worthy of the vein of poetry that the Celts have.—H. G. H.

JULY 6TH, 1907

THE ETON V. HARROW MATCH

SIR,—Permit me to answer "Old Etonian's" letter in your last week's number. As to its taste I say nothing beyond suggesting that the writer has apparently left Eton long enough to have forgotten the manners once supposed to be taught there. If in comparing Eton to the Gentlemen and Harrow to the players "Old Etonian" meant to imply social inferiority, I imagine his letter carries the refutation on the face of it. But if, on the other hand, the implication is that Harrow as the Players know more about the game of cricket and play it better than Eton as the Gentlemen, I should be inclined to agree with him; in proof of which I refer "Old Etonian" to the record of the matches between the two schools and the superior position of Harrow therein.—OLD HARROVIAN

SEPTEMBER 23ʳᵈ, 1901

A PRIMITIVE FERRY

Sɪʀ,—In your issue for October 19ᵀᴴ I see an account of how ponies, etc., are ferried across the channel between Valencia Island and the mainland, and it may interest your readers to know that a similar custom exists at Barmouth in Wales. Although there is a bridge across the Mawddach, it is only used for the railway and for foot passengers. When I was there last summer but one I saw a donkey towed across by a sailing boat. The struggles of the donkey to keep out of the water were hard and prolonged, but it had to give way, and the wind filling the sails, away they went as smoothly as possible.—G. L. Pᴇᴘʟᴇʏ

[We have great pleasure in showing another illustration of a horse crossing the channel between Valencia Island and the mainland, which was omitted when Mr. Fitzgerald's letter was published.—Ed]

"IT MIGHT AMUSE
YOUR READERS
TO KNOW"

*The irrepressible urge to pass on information about oddities
or strange delights has helped fill the correspondence pages
of Country Life since its first publication. One by-product
of this enthusiasm is a particular genre of letter: it's well
known that the undemonstrative Briton will lose his head
when confronted with a tousle-haired pet, and never is this
more clearly demonstrated than in the desire to share the latest
picture of a pet doing the "funniest thing".*

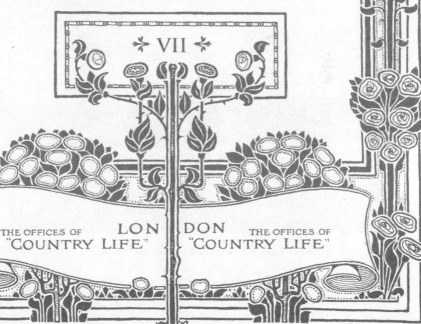

✦ VII ✦

THE OFFICES OF   LONDON   THE OFFICES OF
"COUNTRY LIFE"   "COUNTRY LIFE"

OCTOBER 28ᵀᴴ, 1899

DIVING DOGS

Sɪʀ,—I am indebted to my friend, Mr. R. C. McM. Smyth, of 6, Foster Place, Dublin, for this introduction and the pleasure of writing to you. When showing Mr. Smyth a snap-shot taken of my dog diving off the springboards at the "forty-foot" hole bathing place, Sandy Cove, he said he felt certain you would like to have it for the paper, and I am accordingly sending it to you herewith. The dog is an Irish water spaniel which I have had since he was a wee puppy.—Sᴛᴇᴡᴀʀᴛ C. Sᴛᴜᴅᴅᴇʀᴛ

[It certainly represents a bold leap, and it is very clear and clean cut. It differs, however, from the picture of a diving dog which we showed recently in an essential particular, in that the dog took a real header. In this he is going to come down pretty flat. We are sorry for him, but the Irish water spaniel is a wonderfully tough dog.—Ed]

JULY 22ND, 1916

THE ODDS AGAINST THIRTEEN TRUMPS

This freak single-suit holding is not unknown in bridge games where "goulashes" (or "goolies") are played. A goulash is a variation in which the cards are shuffled and dealt in a manner designed to produce odd distributions. It is still a matter of fierce debate how best to bid on the happy occasion when you hold such a hand.

SIR,—In reply to the question of your correspondent of July 8TH, the chances against thirteen trumps being dealt are 158,750,000,000 to 1, according to Pole.—F. A. G.

MARCH 10TH, 1900

EARWIGS IN THE HOUSE

SIR,—Can any of your readers kindly tell me how to suppress earwigs in my house? They apparently come from the floors at night and are found chiefly on the white paint of the walls and doors, even in the bedrooms. The house is a new one and has no creepers, but was standing half-built for some months.—H. C. L.

DECEMBER 22ND, 1900

COINS IN POTATOES

A spade guinea was an English gold coin minted between 1787 and 1799. On its reverse it bore a device shaped like the spade on playing cards.

SIR,—In the current number of the *Strand Magazine* there is a photograph of a potato in which a halfpenny was found embedded. Herewith I send you a George II farthing, found by my cook in the middle of a large potato which she had pared and cut in two. The farthing was placed almost exactly in the centre, and reposed on a discoloured bed which it had made for itself. How did it get there? Several friends to whom I have referred the matter treated it as a practical joke, but where did the jest come in the shape of a coin so discoloured that its identity could scarcely be discovered, and then only after many cleansings. A scientific acquaintance suggests that the farthing got embedded edgeways on a hard substance and was forced upwards into the growing tuber. Anyway there is the farthing; the potato came from a respectable greengrocer, who tells me that the crop was bought in Kent. Had it been a spade guinea I should not have sent it to you.—H. B. S.

[We have the farthing.—Ed]

NOVEMBER 24TH, 1923

A STRANGE RESURRECTION

SIR,—You may care to publish the enclosed photograph of a beech tree, in view of the astonishing circumstance connected with it. Some time ago it was blown down, the boughs were lopped, and the trunk lay on the ground for some eighteen months. Then one day my forester was going round and nearly had a fit to see the tree standing up again, as in the photograph. We think that heavy rain on the earth among the roots made the base so heavy that it pulled the tree, denuded of branches, up again. It has been standing now for some months. I have never heard of such a thing happening before, but perhaps some of your readers have known such a phenomenon.—POWIS

AUGUST 17TH, 1935

A POLICE STATION IN A TREE

Sir,—In the small town of Gifhorn in North Germany there is a tree, eight hundred years old and perfectly hollow inside. The tree serves as a police station, which gives good shade in summertime. From it the eye of justice watches everything that happens in the neighbourhood.

The entrance to the "station" bears the inscription: "*Dienstraum fuer Ortspolizei*" (Office for local police).—H. S.

AUGUST 22ND, 1908

SELF-SACRIFICE!

SIR,—I was much amused this week by my taxicab driver's argument for a fee over and above his legal fare. He had lost a great deal of time and money in learning to drive, *and all for the sake of the public.*—L. B.

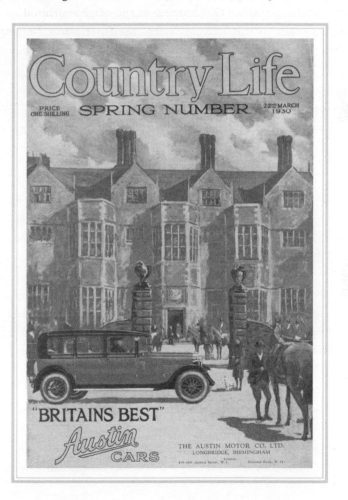

FEBRUARY 23ʳᴰ, 1907

MINDS OTHER THAN OURS

Sɪʀ,—In your issue of January 5ᵀᴴ there is an article by Mr. F. G. Aflalo, which contains the following sentence, "The bray of an ass during its courtship is not, so far as we know, very different from that which it utters before rain, or when getting a thrashing." The popular superstition that the ass brays "before rain" is easily, I think, accounted for, when it is considered that the atmosphere before, during and after rain is in a very favourable condition for the transmission of that "wireless telephony" which the donkeys of a country-side delight to practise; for be it remembered that the donkey is a far more conversational animal than the horse, and that amplitude of voice

"FOR BE IT
REMEMBERED
THAT THE DONKEY
IS A FAR MORE
CONVERSATIONAL
ANIMAL THAN
THE HORSE"

and ear which has called forth the laughter of the witless from time immemorial is merely evidence of the donkey's ancestors having been desert-dwellers, given to inter-communication over vast spaces. There is much individuality and diversity in the voices of donkeys; some there are who, when merely giving greeting to a friend, would lead the uninitiated human hearer to suppose the sound to be the expression of an acute degree of bodily anguish. This brings me to my chief point: Does the donkey raise his voice when "getting a beating"? I hardly think so. Mr. Aflalo's suggestion that it does is the first of the kind that I have ever heard. Has he any evidence to support his assertion? Personally, I am happy to say, I have no data on this point, though I have owned and satisfactorily trained numerous donkeys. I have heard one give a short squeal on many occasions, but that was because she was being made to do what she did not wish, and was suffering rather in mind than in body. Some writer, whose name has escaped me, has specially noticed the silence of the ass under suffering, and has suggested that it is a great pity that this animal is not endowed with the temperament of the pig, who makes the welkin ring with awesome shrieks at the smallest adverse experience. I have seen a donkey, that had been kept a prisoner for some little time, on being turned loose in a field rush madly and fitfully round and about, ears down and tail up, and voice clamorous in a succession of bull-calf-like "bawkings," which I think even Mr. Aflalo would have recognised as differing from the ordinary bray; and one almost ventures to hope that he would have seen in the whole performance some evidence of that intentional playfulness as to the possession of which sense by animals he is so sceptical.—JACQUES L'ANIER

MARCH 9TH, 1907

THE BRAY OF THE ASS

Sir,—Your courteous correspondent is a little hard on me when he thinks that "even" I would have known one note of the ass from another. Yes; I have heard an ass bray loudly when thwacked, and that in this town and not more than a month ago. But I do not pretend to be a very close observer of these animals, and I used the illustration only in passing. In future I shall attend as closely to the ass's braying as I have to your correspondent's letter.—F. G. AFLALO

MAY 7ᵀᴴ, 1921

MUSICAL PHRASE IN BLACKBIRD'S SONG

SIR,—While staying at Buxton last month the attention of my wife and myself was attracted by the following musical phrase in a blackbird's song:

The rest of his song was of the usual inconsequential quality which blackbirds affect ("With his own lonely moods / The blackbird holds a colloquy"). Sometimes he repeated the initial B natural at the end of the phrase, but usually this was omitted. The occurrence of musical phrases in blackbirds' songs has often been noted before. Mr. W. H. Hudson has some fascinating pages upon the subject in his "Adventures Among Birds." He states that the late Mr. C. A. Witchell in his "Evolution of Bird-Song," has recorded in musical notation no fewer than seventy-six blackbird strains. Mr. Hudson thus writes of a blackbird "of genius" he once heard in the New Forest: "This bird did not repeat a strain with some slight variation as is usually the case, but sang differently each time, or varied the strain so greatly as to make it appear like a new melody on each repetition, yet every one of its strains could have been set down in musical notation." Perhaps some of your readers can give other illustrations.—ERNEST BLAKE

NOVEMBER 17TH, 1900

A TAME SQUIRREL

Sir,—I send you a photograph of a pet squirrel belonging to our parlour-maid. He runs loose in the pantry. One day he was lost, and after being called for some time, he popped his head and fore paws up from a jug on a high shelf, looked out and retired again. He often sleeps in this jug, and was lately snapshotted in it.—T. P. R.

NOVEMBER 11TH, 1899

MONSTROUS RABBIT'S TEETH

SIR,—I enclose a photograph of the rabbit, as mentioned in my last letter. It was brought by a carrier of the name of Wilkinson of Burton in Westmorland to Hind and Co., wine merchants, Lancaster. I happened to see the rabbit there, and took a photograph of it. The top teeth were growing backwards into the top of the mouth; the bottom ones, as seen from the photograph, were growing outwards and upwards towards the nostrils. The rabbit was caught by a dog on a farm in Burton, and was in fairly good condition.—T. R. SATTERTHWAITE

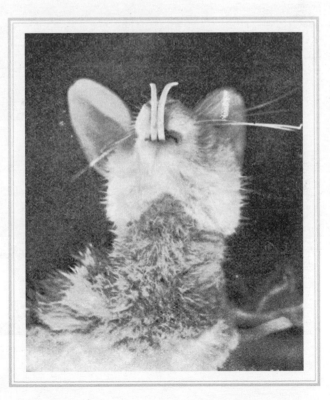

NOVEMBER 11TH, 1899

A DOG WHO PLAYS CROQUET

Sir,—I enclose a snap-shot of an up-to-date terrier who always plays croquet. He enters into the game most thoroughly, though he disregards all rules, and plays on a system of his own with great satisfaction to himself.—E. B.

FEBRUARY 18ᵀᴴ, 1922

A RHINOCEROS AS A PET

SIR,—I send you a photograph of a young rhinoceros about six months of age which was caught last September on Kajaba Plains in East Africa. He weighs 10 st. and is very strong for his size. He fought gallantly before being captured, and it took three natives to bring him into camp. Once he was there, however, he became perfectly tame and affectionate and ran loose about the camp. Later he was taken to a coffee plantation, where he continued to be a most engaging pet.—M. URSULA MIDDLEDITCH

JULY 2ND, 1904

SINGING MICE

SIR,—I should be greatly obliged if you could publish in your correspondence column some particulars regarding singing mice. We had never heard of their existence until a fortnight ago, when we arrived from the Continent, and went into lodgings in an old house just off Oxford Circus. The first night we were woke up by loud singing, as of a number of birds, and our first impression was that someone kept nightingales in cages. The next morning the landlady informed us they were singing mice we had heard, and she had read of them when her lodgers began to hear them in the walls. When we clapped our hands we could hear the mice running away in the walls, and when all was still they began again their concert. It was not squeaking or chirping, but sustained singing, as of canaries in a cage. If you can throw any light on the subject we shall be much pleased, as though we can vouch for what we have heard with our ears, our eyes have not seen the mice, and we are most curious to discover any particulars we can of them.—E. M. JOHNSON

※

AUGUST 28TH, 1920

A CURE FOR GOUT AND RHEUMATISM

SIR,—If any of your readers wish to emulate the robust serenity of health enjoyed by their eighteenth century ancestors, the accompanying cure may be of interest. In the still existing sugar shortage it is also worth noticing that this remedy of asses' milk, according to experiments in nutritive values presented to the French Academy, contained 6.29 per cent of sugar.

Here is a notable cure:

> "In 1681 Sir John Reresby, Bart., M.P. for York, was quite disabled by gout and rheumatism, but, writes Sir John, 'by taking asses' milk first, and cow's milk afterwards, I recovered to a miracle. I must own a great deal to Providence to the discovery of this medicine, milk.'"

By orders of the famous Dr. Mead, Pope drank asses' milk; and in 1753 we find Dr. Fothergill prescribing the same remedy for John Wesley. It seems to have been constantly sold at places of health resort, such as Richmond and Margate, where celebrated "Donkey Hackneyman," Bennett, combined pleasure and medicine for his clients as his advertisement notified:

> "Cow's milk, and Asse's too, I sell,
> And keep a stud for hire,
> Of donkeys, fam'd for going well,
> And mules that never tire."

Children as well as adults participated in the remedy as appears from a school bill of Christmas, 1771:

	£	s.	d.
To Wine, Syrrup, &c. (when ill)	0	1	6
To Asses' Milk	1	5	9
To the Apothecary	0	10	0
	£1	17	3

The old English use of this milk did but carry on classical tradition, for Plutarch tells us that "Asses' milk was commonly used by sick people in the time of Demosthenes."—G. M. GODDEN

LOCAL TYPES

Descriptions and pictures of rural characters constitute a staple of the early correspondence pages of Country Life. Their faithful service, rustic wisdom or craft were understood to be woven in some sense into the very fabric of the British countryside and evidently fascinated readers.

✦ VIII ✦

THE OFFICES OF "COUNTRY LIFE"   LONDON   THE OFFICES OF "COUNTRY LIFE"

SEPTEMBER 23RD, 1899

A SUSSEX CENTENARIAN

SIR,—I send you a photograph of an old shoemaker 100 years and 5 days old, who has all his life led a country life. I enclose a few lines about him.—W. H.

"Rarely indeed do we now meet with a man who has already seen two centuries, but the accompanying picture of 'One hundred – not out' shows a villager who, if he lives until January next, will have seen three centuries, the eighteenth, nineteenth, and twentieth – an almost unique experience. Mr. Thomas Turner, the oldest inhabitant of Balcomlie, an exceedingly pretty village in Mid-Sussex, was six years old when Nelson fell at Trafalgar, and fifteen years old when Wellington and Napoleon met at Waterloo, for he first saw the light on September 1ST, 1799. Curiously enough, he was considered such a delicate baby that he was baptised before he was twenty-four hours old. Yet the 'delicate baby' lived to preside at his own dinner-table, in the cottage he has occupied for seventy-seven years, on September 1ST, 1899, and see around him two sons, five daughters, a dozen grandchildren, one great-great-grandson, and numerous other relatives. When still a boy he was apprenticed as a stonemason, but an injury through a fall caused him to change his

trade, and he became a shoemaker, and worked at that trade until he had passed his ninetieth birthday, when he retired. His 100TH birthday aroused much enthusiasm, for rich and poor alike came to congratulate him, letters and telegrams from far and near came pouring in, and even the bells of the old parish church were set ringing. In talking to him he recalled many incidents of the good old smuggling days, of the robbers who hid in the forests, of the awfully messy Sussex roads, of the women riding on pillions behind their husbands, the first passenger train, and many other old-time events and customs. The venerable old man is still enjoying good health, and his friends wish him many happy returns of the day."

NOVEMBER 9ᵀᴴ, 1907
A CHILD OF NATURE

Country Life *magazine never could resist a story about gipsies and its correspondents, with varying degrees of sympathy, were never slow to join the debate.*

Sɪʀ,—Your leading article last week showed such an insight into, and sympathy with, the gipsy's life that I venture to hope that the accompanying photograph may be of interest. The picturesqueness of the little lass in the bracken by the roadside will appeal to the artist and the sentimentalist, while, on the other hand, the stern economist and game preserver will find in her rags and (probably) defective education a text on which to found unanswerable arguments against those "poaching pests" of the country-side – the gipsies, justification for whose existence, he will say, it is hard to perceive in 1907.—N.

SEPTEMBER 20TH, 1902

THE VILLAGE COBBLER

SIR,—I enclose a photograph which you may think suitable for publication in your series of "Village Types" – the village snob, an old shoemaker eighty-five years old. He tells me he does not make many boots now, but considers his little shop a "Home for Incurables," patching and mending not being such heavy work for one of his age.—B. W. Z. WRIGHT

OCTOBER 8ᵀᴴ, 1898

AN UNDISTRESSED IRISHMAN

SIR,—So much has been said and written lately on the subject of distress among the Irish peasantry in the West of Ireland, that I cannot help thinking it will be quite a pleasant change to see the accompanying photograph taken from life of an undistressed Irish peasant. Old Pat Murray has been a familiar figure for many years in the neighbourhood of Killala and

"HE EARNS AN HONEST LIVELIHOOD BY HAWKING HIS FISH"

Ballina, where he earns an honest livelihood by hawking his fish. One would naturally suppose that the Killala fishermen supply him with his well-filled panniers. Not so; the inhabitants of that picturesque old town above the wide bay are not sufficiently fond of exerting themselves, and would rather spend their days for the most part in gazing at the sea than in trying to reap any of its rich harvest. All the fish sold by the old man is taken in Lacken Bay, about six miles beyond Killala and twelve from Ballina. The venerable pony and his quaint companion are always welcome sights, and at my home, where his portrait was taken, he is invariably well received, given food and rest, and a good price for his fish. In these days, when so much is heard about the "disthressful counthry," it is as well to know that there is another side to the question, though it does not generally appear in print, and old Murray is a living example of it – a cheerful, hard-working, and consequently undistressed Irishman.—A. M. SAUNDERS KNOX-GORE

JUNE 13TH, 1925

ARGYLLSHIRE GIPSIES

SIR,—As speed is counted in the Highlands, we had travelled fast that early spring morning covering thirty miles since leaving our last village, without sighting a living soul. In such conditions the most cautious driver grows careless of anything beyond keeping his car on the narrow track – and generally even that is done for him automatically by the ruts. We had turned into Glen Etive and were making fair speed along the track shown here, when suddenly, rushing along one of the innumerable switchbacks that are such a feature of Highland roads, we almost ran down this little family of wanderers. Gipsies are a very familiar feature of the Scottish landscape. The common impression of them is gained from the frequent sight of their camps, where all the work is being done by the women, while the men sit round the fire, their swarthy skins, gloomy looks and habit of huddling close together giving a sinister appearance to the group. They practise a variety of trades, of which metal-working has always been the principal one. Formerly it took the form of shoeing, and there was a time when, in south-east Europe, no one could equal the gipsy's skill at this art. Now, in Scotland, the making and mending of pots and pans is their chief trade, and nine out of ten families belong to the fraternity of the bit and solder. Tinkers, or "tinkler bodies," as they are called in Scotland, are specialists, and in the remote country districts specialists in a service in such common demand are handsomely patronised and often do a roaring trade. The family in our picture will shortly reach the summit of attainment in gipsydom when they purchase a two-wheel cart to hitch to the pony.—E. M. WRIGHT

OCTOBER 30TH, 1926

THE SHEPHERD UP-TO-DATE

SIR,—The enclosed photograph illustrates forcibly, I think, the almost universal use to which motor vehicles are put nowadays. Every day this Perthshire shepherd and his two collies, Sailor and Jock, proceed in this fashion to the grazing ground some half-dozen miles away. Immediately the motor combination is brought out from its garage the "twa dugs" take their place in the sidecar and evince great eagerness to be off. That they enjoy their daily joy-ride none who has seen them will deny. Passers along the Mollands road near Callander are much intrigued by the unusual spectacle.—HAMISH MUIR

DECEMBER 31ST, 1921

A POETIC BLACKSMITH

SIR,—This entertaining blacksmith's shop is on the Great North Road at Cromwell. On the board above the door is this inscription:

"F. Naylor,
Blacksmith.
Gentlemen as you pass by
Upon this shoe pray cast an eye.
If it be too strait
I'll make it wider.
I'll ease the Horse & please the rider.
If lame from shoeing, as they often are
You may have them eased with the greatest care."

—J. DENTON ROBINSON

MAY 19ᵀᴴ, 1923

A VANISHING TRADE

Sɪʀ,—The crow-scarer is a vanishing character of the countryside. His familiar and joyous shout of "Carr whoo" and the rattle of his "clappers" to frighten the birds off the cornfields is now rarely heard. And change has overtaken him where he still flourishes. Are there not military puttees, relics of the Great War, to be seen on the young gentleman of the trade whose photograph I am sending to you?—A. L. Bᴏɴᴀs

SEPTEMBER 25TH, 1926

FROM WEST YORKSHIRE

SIR,—Readers of Mr. Cutcliffe-Hyne's excellent story, "Ben Watson," will be just now particularly interested in the dalesmen; so I send you a photograph of one, a typical dweller in the Fell country of West Yorkshire.—G. CROWTHER

NOVEMBER 9TH, 1901

A WELSH VILLAGE TYPE

SIR,—I fancy that in Wales we have types of men and women as old and curious even as those you have shown from the Orkney Islands. The one whose photograph I enclose is a Laugharne (Carmarthenshire) cockle-woman, and I greatly regret to say that the picturesque costume in which she appears, and which once was so prevalent, is now fast dying out. The cockle-women wore divided skirts, as this one does, long before that convenient article of feminine attire was thought of by their fashionable sisters in town. Of her wooden clogs and her basket, her round hat and her shawl, I forbear to speak. Why I do not like to see old forms of dress getting lost is that their doing so tends to increase that dull monotony of which you spoke some time back, and is perfectly fatal to the expression of individuality. You could not really tell some of our Welsh fisher-girls now from milliners, typewriters, or pupil-teachers.—TAFFY

> "I GREATLY REGRET TO SAY THAT THE PICTURESQUE COSTUME IN WHICH SHE APPEARS, AND WHICH ONCE WAS SO PREVALENT, IS NOW FAST DYING OUT"

FEBRUARY 15TH, 1902

SCOTTISH VILLAGE TYPES

SIR,—In supplement to the article you wrote for us some time ago, you may like to reproduce the enclosed photograph of a Highland crofter from Skye. The rugged face is a very typical one indeed, telling of hardship and long labour by land and sea, with plenty of hints in it too of the strict dogmatic Presbyterianism prevalent among this class, and conveying an idea of equally dogmatic Radicalism, more characteristic of the old school perhaps than the new.

I think you ought to admire his capacious raiment and particularly the home-knitted Tam-o'-shanter cap. At his side is the big pot, or "yetlin,"

"THOSE POOR FOLK WHO EXTRACT A SCANTY LIVELIHOOD FROM LAND AND SEA"

fit alike for boiling porridge and pig's-meat. The house of stone and thatch, windowless and uncomfortable, is such as many a crofter has to dwell in. A picture of abject poverty it will probably be pronounced, and yet what an eloquent picture might be made for the greater treasuring of those poor folk who extract a scanty livelihood from land and sea and yet live open-air healthy lives, and produce far more vigorous children than spring from the streets. I think there is even an Imperial reason for protecting them, since these people, born in hearing of the breakers, quite naturally take to a seafaring life and become our best sailors. It is good for the fagged man of business to have a grouse moor, but it is better that the crofter should have his means of livelihood preserved.—G. A.

APRIL 8ᵀᴴ, 1922

A DANGER TO CORACLE FISHING

Sɪʀ,—The most ancient form of fishing, that carried on in coracles, is threatened with extinction by a new Bill which comes before Parliament shortly. These pictures show the coracle fishermen at Cenarth, near Cardigan, on the river Tivy. The coracle is a craft used by the ancient Britons, and is made with strips of willow, covered with calico, and painted with hot tar. This boat is only used to-day by the fishermen on the rivers in West Wales. The threatening clause

"THE MOST ANCIENT FORM OF FISHING"

is No. 61 of the Salmon and Freshwater Fisheries Bill, which empowers fishery boards to restrict the number of net licences issued, also to select the individuals to whom such licences shall be issued. The men are energetically protesting that this is an infringement of rights they and their ancestors have enjoyed for centuries.—Hᴀʀᴏʟᴅ Sǫᴜɪʙʙs

MARCH 9TH, 1907

THE "LITTLE PEOPLE"

SIR,—The following tale of fairies told to me more than twenty years ago in Ireland may interest your readers: Fishing one day from a boat on Lough Derg I enquired of the boatmen if they had ever seen fairies. At first, fearing to be laughed at, they scorned the idea; but when they realised it was a genuine enquiry, and not an intention to poke fun at

> "PROBABLY IT WAS A FANTASY OF MISTY EXHALATION FROM THE FIELD"

them, one of them told the following: On a Sunday he was returning after Mass, and stood with a friend, named Sullivan, on the bridge of Killaloe. Looking towards a potato-field on the slope of the rising ground to the east of the town, a field which he was able to point out from the boat, he saw issuing from the liss a troop of little people, one being distinctly taller than the rest. At first they seemed rather blurred, then took distinct shapes, and began to play the national game of hurley among the bare potato rigs. He called Sullivan's attention to them, but for some time his friend could not see them, then said he could, and they watched the game together for a time. Then the sun went in, and the fairies, moving towards the liss, as if returning to it, vanished. Probably it was a fantasy of misty exhalation from the field, but it shows how strong the belief in the little people is in Ireland. Lisses, which are so common in the fields there, are rough pieces, sometimes hillocks, sometimes depressions, often bushy, but never cultivated. I have been told they are left as doorways for the fairies when visiting the earth's surface.—ALFRED C. E. WELBY

APRIL 19TH, 1941

TRICYCLE CRIER

SIR,—I enclose a photograph of the town crier at the Sussex village of Selsey, whose position is believed to be unique in at least two respects.

First, he is said to be the only crier in the country to travel round making his cries on a tricycle. Dressed in scarlet tunic and waistcoat and a top hat, and clanging his bell, he goes as far as four miles out of the district in this way.

He is thought also to be the only freelance crier to hold an official appointment. Villagers officially appointed him because of the large number of announcements which have to be made, but he is paid by whoever employs him at the time at the rate of 5s. a cry.

Then Selsey believes that she is the only village left to have a crier.— NORMAN WYMER, ANCHOR LANE, WORTHING

COUNTRY CHILDHOOD

The early letters pages convey a wealth of information about the upbringing and pleasures of Victorian and Edwardian children in the countryside. In some respects, their freedom seems enviable today but there were responsibilities and experiences that a modern child might baulk at.

※ IX ※

THE OFFICES OF   LONDON   THE OFFICES OF
"COUNTRY LIFE"   "COUNTRY LIFE"

A CHARMING PICTURE

Lady Mostyn presents her compliments to the editor of COUNTRY LIFE, and encloses a photograph of her little boy, Charles Pyers Mostyn, taken in his carriage, which was made by Joseph Parsons, Avongoch, Holywell.

[It is a charming picture, and the little carriage does great credit to the Holywell builder.—Ed]

SEPTEMBER 28ᵀᴴ, 1907

PUNCH AND JUDY SHOWS

Sɪʀ,—I think the accompanying photograph of a Punch and Judy show may be of interest to your readers. These amusing puppet-shows, which are, unfortunately, becoming rarer every year, travel usually in country districts, though recently a very clever one has been visiting different parts of London and attracting large and enthusiastic crowds. It may not be generally known that the word punch is a contraction of punchinello, which is itself a corruption of pulcinello, the droll character in Neapolitan comedy. The origin of the character is veiled in obscurity, but the drama of Punch and Judy as now known is attributed to Silvio Fiorillo, an Italian comedian who lived in the seventeenth century. Later on in the same century it was introduced into this country, where it very soon established itself in popular favour. It is a great pity that these shows, which abound with wit and humour, should now be met with so rarely.—D. G.

DECEMBER 28TH, 1907

BLIND-MAN'S BUFF
IN MANY LANDS

Sir,—Now that Christmas is upon us, and that all right-minded people will be eating plain pudding and playing blind-man's buff – or, perhaps, will be seeing pictures in the Christmas fire of games of blind-man's bluff played sixty years ago – the question asks itself: Why should this game of all others belong to the Old English Christmas? Perhaps the classic example of the Christmas "blind-man" is that of Mr. Pickwick, in the kitchen of Dingley Dell Farm, where old Wardle and his family, his guests, his servants and even the farm hands gathered on Christmas Eve, "observed by old Wardle's forefathers from time immemorial." With which vision of Mr. Pickwick in spectacles keeping up the Old English Christmas blindfolded, we may leave the age of coat tails and speckled silk stockings, to find our next blind-man in Gay's charming verses, verses written in the days of Beau Brocade:

"As once I play'd at blind man's-buff it hap't,
  About my eyes the towel thick was wrapt.
  I mui'd the swains, and seie'd on Blouxelind.
  True speaks that ancient proverb, 'Love is blind.'"

Passing over another hundred years, the old game suddenly emerges into history, for it is recorded of the great Gustavus Adolphus that at the very time when he was proving himself the scourge of the House of Austria, and when in the midst of his triumphs, he would amuse himself with playing blind-man's buff with his colonels. Gustavus brings us to the seventeenth century, but our own Henry VIII is reputed inadvertently to have caused great popularity for the game by his treatment of Wolsey. The game then bore the name of Hoodman Blind, and it is clear that the players used the hoods of the period both as a means for blinding the "blind-man," and also as knotted instruments with which to buffet him or her. The illumination showing the ladies of the period playing "Hoodman blind" is particularly charming, with the vigorous figure of the blind-man, with kilted up skirt, ready for action. It is interesting to note that in the old comedy called "Two Angry Women of Abington" the game is called the "Christmas-sport of Hobman Blind." A pedigree of 700 years seems a quite respectable record for a Christmas game; but that is but a mere fraction of the "life-history" of blind-man's buff.

The ancient author Verelius supposes that the Ostrogoths introduced the game into Italy, where it is called *giucco della cieca*, or the play of the blind. We know that it was in use among the Romans; and it was, says Dr. Jamieson, not unknown to the Greeks.

In Iceland the game was known as *drakis blinda*, and one illustration shows that Mr. Pickwick has his Corean analogue. For "here, drawn

by the pen and brush of a native Corean artist, we may see Corean boys and girls playing what we fondly think of as our own supremely English game of blind-man's buff."—G. M. G.

WAR HELPERS IN THE VILLAGE

Sɪʀ,—Possibly you may consider these photographs of sufficient interest to appear in COUNTRY LIFE. The first is of village children learning to spin; they are here seen spinning wool for knitting into bed-socks for the wounded. The second is of the mascot goat of the 97ᵀᴴ Field Company Royal Engineers, which contributed towards the supply of milk for a cheese making demonstration by Miss Olive Rawson at an exhibition of village industries opened by Lady Cowdray at Byfleet on May 1ˢᵀ, the proceeds of which were devoted to the Star and Garter Fund.—A. G. S.

DECEMBER 3RD, 1898

AMATEUR MILKMAIDS

SIR,—I send you herewith a photograph of my youngest sisters as amateur milkmaids. I think you will agree that they seem to appreciate country life.—E. WILKINSON

STARTING WELL

Sir,—I think you may like the enclosed snap-shot for your paper of a small friend of mine, aged seven years, "ready for the front," and anxious to serve his Queen and country. At the time of taking he was in the act of putting his elder brother, aged nine, through his facings. He is a fine little fellow, and, judging by his air of importance, might be Commander-in-Chief.—Richard Amble

OCTOBER 10ᵀᴴ, 1914

TOO OLD FOR THE NAVY AT FIFTEEN!

Sɪʀ,—During the school holidays my boy of fifteen has given me more than one uncomfortable hour. When he was younger and of an age to enter Osborne he very much wanted to go into the Navy. In a time of "piping peace," I, like other fathers in a similar position, carefully considered the material prospect.

> "IF A SCRAP OF RED TAPE IS TO STAND IN THE WAY OF SECURING FOR THE COUNTRY'S SERVICE THE FLOWER OF OUR YOUTH"

A passion for the sea is common enough at the age of thirteen, and is liable to die down later. But these considerations count for very little now that war is upon us, and the first consideration is how best to serve the country. The boy feels this strongly; is, in fact, full of reproaches for not being allowed to follow his bent. I now agree with his ambition, and would be only too glad to let him enter the Navy if it were possible. Only under the present regulations it seems that a boy is too old at fifteen! Many professional men are in the same position as myself, and it seems to be worth considering if a scrap of red tape is to stand in the way of securing for the country's service the flower of our youth. Here is the situation at a glance. On every hand the best of our young men are applying for commissions in the Army, and for them there is immediate and pressing need. So far little has been said about filling the inevitable gaps that will be made in the ranks of officers in the Senior Service. My suggestion is that the Admiralty should revert, for a time, to its past practice of taking older boys who could be made ready to serve afloat more quickly than if the present system is followed rigidly. Even from the naval standpoint these older boys, because of their Public School education, will not be far behind boys of similar age who have spent some time at Osborne, and they would soon recover any lost ground. When I remember how much controversy the existing age limit has provoked in naval circles, I am bold to make the suggestion that the Admiralty should now open the door of the Navy to older boys. The new regulations for the special entry of naval cadets allow some to be admitted between the ages of seventeen and a half and eighteen and a half, i.e., at the age when they normally leave their Public Schools. Under this rule they presumably have very little, if any, training at Dartmouth, as much of their one and a half years' course has to be passed on a cruiser. By my proposal the younger Public School boy could have a normal and full training at Dartmouth, omitting only the preliminary work at Osborne, which is, in effect, only general education. Our strong First Lord has always shown readiness to make immediate and drastic alterations when the interests of the State have demanded them, and I hope he will give the proposal the serious consideration which my friends tell me it deserves.—PATER

A REFORMED CHARACTER

Sɪʀ,—In view of incidents which have led to certain aspersions being made upon my character, I venture to let you know that I have decided to turn over a new leaf. I enclose a photograph of myself in my new situation.—Aʟsᴀᴛɪᴀɴ

SEPTEMBER 17ᵀᴴ, 1898

A CONTRAST

Sɪʀ,—With this letter I send you a photograph, taken in my farmyard, you may like to reproduce among your country scenes in your excellent paper. The stallion is perhaps interesting as exhibiting the triumph of mind over matter.—Lᴇᴏɴᴀʀᴅ Nᴏʙʟᴇ

DECEMBER 2ND, 1933

CHRISTMAS IN SHETLAND

SIR,—Not all the Shetland Islands observe the same calendar. Some keep modern time; some are twelve days behind it. Some keep New Year's Day as Christmas; others, using the old calendar, are twelve days behind that. So, altogether, the festive season is a kind of continuous performance.

Surrounded by the sea, the Shetlands enjoy a most even temperature, and during the two festive seasons I was there the outdoor conditions were good. And outdoor conditions mean a great deal to the Shetlanders' Christmas, for a gale of fury may mean no Christmas mail, no Christmas turkey from Aberdeen, and no expected friends from some of the other islands.

"THE CHILDREN TAKE PART IN THEIR ANNUAL EVENT OF GUISING"

Christmas is the great occasion when the children take part in their annual event of guising. This performance is taken very seriously.

Every school child is found on the streets of Lerwick on the afternoon of Christmas Eve. And they are so arrayed that even their own mothers would not know them beneath those fantastic masks and in those strange costumes of many colours. Thus disguised, they go from door to door and from shop to shop. They speak in unnatural voices to keep up the illusion, and their usual formula is "Have you got anything for me to-night?"

And a large bag is held out for the reception of oranges, apples, nuts, or any other commodity you care to offer. And if you give them coppers they will appreciate it all the more. The wise shopkeeper opens a barrel of apples or a case of oranges. And the wise householder sends to the bank for ten shillingsworth of coppers; for it is a most serious breach of Christmas etiquette to send any one child empty away.

When the children have finished, it is the turn of the adults. They, too, issue forth to "guise." They do not come to beg, they come to entertain. Any Tom, Dick, or Harry in the town may walk into your house with you quite ignorant of his identity. He will probably come in with a girl, also disguised; and they will carry on a conversation in affected speech.

It is your job to guess who it is that is visiting. And after a few guesses, which may be right or wrong, the guisers unmask and you see to whom you have been speaking. Cake and wine is then the order of the night, the usual greetings are exchanged, compliments given, and you are left in peace until the next party arrives.

The Shetlanders are most superstitious, and if, perchance, a minister of religion accompanies them on a fishing expedition they will, they believe, toil all night and take nothing. I had gone on board to see a friend, and quite unconsciously I had brought with me trouble. My visit meant a most disastrous Christmas. The clerical collar on the fishing boat had taken all the luck away.—ARTHUR T. RICH

OCTOBER 12TH, 1901

A TAME LION CUB

SIR,—Here are some photographs taken lately of a young lion which will perhaps interest some of your readers. This lion was found at birth by the Count Joseph Potocki whilst on a shooting expedition in the Blue Nile at the beginning of this year. It is now rather more than seven months old, and is the constant companion and playfellow of the Count's two sons; it is left free to roam about the grounds, and when it cannot have the children to play with, it romps with the Scotch collie, as you can see in the photograph, or with the two dwarfs who are in the Count's service. At first it was brought up with great care, but now it is a splendid specimen of a sturdy young lion.—N. M.

> "WHEN IT CANNOT HAVE THE CHILDREN TO PLAY WITH, IT ROMPS WITH THE SCOTCH COLLIE OR WITH THE TWO DWARFS WHO ARE IN THE COUNT'S SERVICE"

THE GENTLEMAN ABROAD

The cult of the gentleman and lady adventurer has lived long in the pages of Country Life. Travellers with the means and time sent to the editor some extraordinary photographs and reports from across the globe.

✦ X ✦

THE OFFICES OF   LON DON   THE OFFICES OF
"COUNTRY LIFE"   "COUNTRY LIFE"

FEBRUARY 23RD, 1907

A SCENE IN PALESTINE

SIR,—I am sending you a panoramic photograph taken by me in Palestine last autumn, which I hope you may think interesting enough to publish in COUNTRY LIFE. From Nazareth we drove to Tiberias, and this photograph was taken while watering the horses at a spring outside Cana in Galilee. The Bedouin's mare is drinking from a trough made from an ancient sarcophagus. The village is surrounded by a hedge of prickly pear.—A. ETHEL WARD

DECEMBER 4ᵀᴴ, 1926

THE BEAR AS A HIGHWAYMAN

Sɪʀ,—The photographs I enclose show peaceful penetration on the part of a bear which emerged from the forest in the Canadian Rockies in September last as two motorists were passing in their car. In the first, a piece of chocolate has been thrown to the bear, which he is about to eat. The second shows how the bear, having smelt more chocolate, has sprung on the car to demand it, and the chauffeur is in the act of giving him a piece more. In the last, not having been given all the chocolate, the bear has sprung on to the hood of the car to demand the rest of it. This so frightened the lady in the car that she threw the remainder of the chocolate, still wrapped up in its paper, on to the road behind the car, and so got rid of the bear, which then retired into the forest. Most of the Canadian Rocky Mountains are in a National Game Reserve several hundred square miles in area, within which space no shooting of animals is allowed. Although the bears are wild, they are not savage, nor are they dangerous unless molested. The two motorists were travelling through the heart of the Rocky Mountains from Banff to Windermere.—W. R. F.

OCTOBER 16TH, 1920

A TITWILLOW TRAGEDY

SIR,—A thousand years ago there was a fair Court lady named Miss Uneme in the ancient capital of Nara, Japan, who enjoyed for many years the special attention of the Mikado. In later years she found to her extreme sorrow that he would not treat her with so much favour as before, and so, driven to despair, she left the palace in the dead of night and killed herself by throwing her body into the pond Sarusawa that is shown in the picture. The pond is still now attracting the visitors, and they all take delight in looking at the beautiful goldfish in the pond. Notice a girl in the picture pointing out a big fish to her little sister.—KIYOSHI SAKAMOTO

JANUARY 26ᵀᴴ, 1901

A BELGIAN BRAKE

SIR,—In travelling through Belgium, and especially in the district of which the famous Grotte de Han is the centre, one is struck by the fact that the brakes of almost all the conveyances are protected by an old shoe, in the manner shown in the accompanying photograph, which perhaps you may like to reproduce in your interesting journal.—ANGLO-SAXON

JULY 26ᵀᴴ, 1902

THE END OF AN ANCIENT MONUMENT

The collapse of the iconic bell tower in 1902 captured the international imagination, and was a key factor in creating the abiding fear that Venice's eventual fate is to subside into the lagoon.

SIR,—At this moment, when all lovers of Venice are mourning with her over the collapse of her beautiful Campanile, it may interest your readers to see the exact manner in which the great monument fell. It is touching, too, to read in the Venetian papers – Conservative and Radical alike – how the dominant note is that of sorrow over the bell-tower that for more than a thousand years has shared in the joys, the griefs, the triumphs,

the reverses of the city; and of admiration over consideration shown by the belfry in its collapse. *"Xe casca el Campanil,"* exclaim the inhabitants in their soft dialect, and forthwith they point out how thoughtful up to the end the grand old building had been. It claimed no sacrifice of human life; it refrained from injuring its colleagues in art and history – the Basilica of St. Mark and the Palace of the Doges. It sank to rest, overwhelmed with the weight of years and honours, carrying with it to the grave the respect, the admiration, the love of all the civilised world, and leaving a sense of personal loss that for this generation at least can never pass away.—A. W.

DECEMBER 6ᵀᴴ, 1902

A PUNJABI FISHERMAN

SIR,—It is not often that we associate the inhabitants of India with a love of sport, except, perhaps, big-game shooting and polo. The enclosed photograph is a portrait of a Punjabi fisherman. He is very keen about the sport, and his fine dignified figure is well known to nearly everyone who has fished in the river Mahl near Poonah.—C. G. R., PESHAWAR

NOT SANTA CLAUS

SIR,—I should imagine that few big towns in any part of the globe possess such a picturesque figure as a road-sweeper as does Innsbruck, in the old gentleman in my photograph.

His green jacket, "plus fours" and hat bedecked with feathers set off his snow-white Santa Claus beard to advantage. He was obviously proud of his lowly job. Every movement with broom and shovel was dignified to a degree. Of me, a mere foreign sightseer, he took not the slightest notice, in spite of the rather obvious camera. Surely a greater contrast than this fine old fellow and the modern tram-lined streets of Innsbruck could hardly be imagined.—H. T. COMERFORD

DECEMBER 2ND, 1933

AT HUNGARIAN CROSS-ROADS

SIR,—In a country as flat at Hungary, cross-roads are for the most part easily visible, and so mean little danger to the motorist. There is, however, one entirely "blind "crossing on the way from Budapest to Siofok on Lake Balaton. This road has a splendid surface, and, Balaton being Hungary's "seaside", carries a lot of fast traffic. At this spot, in place of the usual

international sign, the authorities have put up the striking warning shown in the illustration. Exigencies of lighting made it impossible to take the photograph from the front, but the doggerel legend on the board runs:

LASSU HAJTAS VAGY

GYASZSZERTARTAS

which, literally translated, means "Drive slowly or a funeral procession." The effigy of the driver, hanging dead over the steering wheel, his head and neck liberally smeared with red paint, adds a touch of realism well calculated to arrest the attention and slacken the pace of any passing motorist.—S. V. CONWAY

OCTOBER 8TH, 1927

SAFETY FIRST IN PERU

SIR,—Beside the main road between Callao and Lima there stands on a pedestal a wrecked Ford car minus its engine, with its front wheels attached to the chassis by chains. The inscription *"Despacio se va lejos"* means "Slowly one goes far." It has been put there as a warning to passing motorists, since there have been many accidents in the neighbourhood.—C. UCHTER KNOX

DESPACIO SE
VA LEJOS

SEPTEMBER 8ᵀᴴ, 1923

A BAMBOO BRIDGE

SIR,—The enclosed photograph of a Lisu bridge on the Burma–China frontier may interest you. It is made entirely of bamboo, and spans the Ta-ho, a small tributary of the Irrawaddy, which rises in Yunnan. Mules, of course, cannot cross here, but are compelled to ford the river two miles higher up. Ten years ago the merchants of T'eng-yueh were talking of building a proper bridge here, to carry the traffic and facilitate direct communication with the Burma railway. Ten years hence they will doubtless still be discussing it. The result is that most of the trade between Burma and Yunnan still goes through Bhamo, which is not on the railway. The steep curve of the bridge makes it very slippery, and the European is advised to remove his boots before crossing. The footway is made of two bamboos lashed together, one springing from either bank. The Lisu are a hill tribe scattered all up the Burma–China frontier.—F. KINGDON WARD

Also Available in the Series

Curious Observations

A COUNTRY MISCELLANY

"A wonderful reminder of our traditions, our country customs, that it is now, more than ever, important to guard"
Julian Fellowes

The Glory of the Garden

A HORTICULTURAL CELEBRATION

"If you can resist reading these pieces then you are not the sort of person I hope to find myself sitting next to at the dinner table"
Alan Titchmarsh

Gentlemen's Pursuits

A COUNTRY MISCELLANY
FOR THE DISCERNING

Tips on pipe-smoking, advice on gun dogs and the last word in how to cut a dash – everything the perfect gentleman needs.